The 5-Day Job Search

The 5-Day Job Search

Proven Strategies to Answering Tough Interview Questions & Getting Multiple Job Offers

Annie Margarita Yang

Annie Yang Financial

BOSTON, MA

Annie Yang Financial Corporation
P.O. Box 505149 Chelsea, MA 02150-5149
annieyangfinancial.com
annie@annieyangfinancial.com

Library of Congress Control Number: 2023911930

Hardcover ISBN: 978-1-961039-00-1
Paperback ISBN: 978-1-961039-01-8
eBook ISBN: 978-1-961039-02-5
Audiobook ISBN: 978-1-961039-03-2

Editing by Tippy Felzenstein
Interior Design by Jenny Yang
Book Cover Design by Luis Guadalupe

Dedicated to my high school guidance counselor,
Mrs. Garcia:

"By choosing not to go straight to college, the only destiny for you is failure."

These words echoed in my head throughout my high school years, as you relentlessly instilled this belief in me.

My dreams began as a fragile candle flame, and for the past ten years, I've used your disheartening words as fuel, pouring them onto my fire like gasoline.

All I ever wanted was to prove you wrong.

Whenever I felt like giving up, thoughts of you drove me forward. Though I once harbored deep resentment, I now realize that your doubt was my greatest blessing. Had everyone around me simply praised my intelligence and predicted success, I might have grown complacent and failed to push myself beyond my limits. Talent alone is never enough.

So, Mrs. Garcia, I can finally say: thank you!

Contents

Foreword

This book is about preparing yourself for a life that will open any door you wish in five days. If you belong to the top 20%, you will take this book seriously, committing to the workbook until you can add your own story of landing a job in five days. If you are among the 5% of that 20%, you will surpass this book's content and shine your light brighter than you can currently imagine.

As you embark on this journey, maintain a record of your progress. As Annie put it, "Take notes." You'll be grateful you did. The truth is that anyone can succeed if they apply themselves. Indeed, 100% of you can rise to the top of the global population. The fact that you are reading this book is proof that you qualify.

Read every word twice. Do it exactly as described or better, but just do it!

Annie has provided all the resources you need. Don't let them go to waste.

This book is for those willing to do what it takes, even if you initially believe you can't.

Tippy Felzenstein
Life Coach & Book Editor
Author of Wake Up And Plan For Roses: Discover The Hidden Magic Within Your Subconscious Reality
Host of Tippy Talk Show

Preface

I'm not one to boast about my achievements at work; I prefer to let my work speak for itself. In real life, I don't mention that I'm a YouTuber, an author, or a company owner. When asked to introduce myself, I simply say, "I'm an accountant."

I don't identify with Instagram influencers who constantly travel and showcase endless new outfits. I believe people shouldn't follow me in that manner. My only social media presence consists of a personal Facebook for real-life friends and a YouTube channel where I share content that I believe will genuinely improve someone's life. I created an Instagram and Twitter to claim the username handle, but that's all.

One night, as I tried to sleep, persistent voices in my head wouldn't stop talking. They insisted I write a new book and detailed exactly what to include. Exhausted, I told them to quiet down and come back in the morning. However, they dismissed my pleas, emphasizing the urgency and utmost importance of publishing this book. My intention was to grow my accounting practice—not become a career coach and write a second book. I urged them to find someone else for the task, but they insisted I was the only one capable of doing it. I relented and jotted down their ideas until I finally slept at 4:00 am.

The same scenario played out the following night. The voices continued for ten days, dictating the entire manuscript. When I later read other books on job hunting, I discovered that my work was wholly original. Other books tend to have similar advice and writing styles because their authors research existing material before paraphrasing and adding their spin.

While there is some overlapping information in this book, its content is unique since it is based solely on my personal experiences and learning over the past ten years. I only recommend strategies that I have tested myself, so rest assured that everything I ask of you is possible to achieve. In fact, you can accomplish the same results faster than I did since I had no system to follow and had to learn through trial and error.

By blazing the trail and sharing my experiences in this book for less than $20, I hope to help you propel your career forward.

Many blessings.

Acknowledgments

In 2015, when I was 20 years old, my ex-boyfriend committed a crime and went to jail. Due to his family's political connections, the district attorney advised him to cease contact with me, effectively ending our relationship. He had been my only source of emotional support, and without any friends, I was left devastated.

Determined to pick up the pieces and rebuild my life, I joined Toastmasters with the goal of improving my public speaking skills and eventually sharing my story from a position of power. It was at Toastmasters that I met Tippy Felzenstein, who would become my life coach. I struggled with the fact that all my friends went to college right after high school, while I carved my own path, facing disapproval from many rational adults.

Tippy believed in my potential and shared invaluable wisdom, helping me view my challenges from a fresh perspective. She nurtured me like a seed. Whenever I didn't believe in myself and felt scared, I called her for advice. When I told her I didn't think I could make more money, she doubled down that I could make more money than I could ever imagine and that I just didn't see it yet. Whenever I had a problem with someone at work, she taught me how to navigate the situation. She also held me accountable on a weekly basis for three years straight, ensuring I made steady progress toward my goals. Tippy's support was instrumental in shaping the person I am today.

I want to express my gratitude to Tippy not only for her role as my life coach but also for editing this book. Her involvement strengthened the manuscript since she witnessed firsthand the journey I took to achieve my current success. Additionally, I would like to thank Brian Rapsey, Bea Guzman, and Heritage Akangbe for beta reading and providing invaluable feedback. I am grateful to my sister, Jenny Yang, for formatting the book for print and eBook publication and Luis Guadalupe for designing the cover.

I could not have accomplished everything I have without the support of these incredible individuals. Creating exceptional products and services, including this book, requires a team effort. Thank you all for your contributions.

Discover Clarity and Purpose

Personal and Spiritual Growth with Tippy Felzenstein, empathic and spiritually-rooted guidance.

1. Gain Clarity: Develop a better understanding of your true desires and goals, empowering you to make informed decisions and pursue meaningful paths in life.
2. Overcome Challenges: Learn to face and resolve life's obstacles and difficult situations with resilience, grace, and confidence.
3. Personal Development: Recognize and understand your strengths and weaknesses.
4. Action Planning: Create a tailored action plan, which can be converted into a business plan, providing a clear roadmap to achieve your objectives.
5. Skill Enhancement: Identify your existing skills and areas for growth.
6. Inner Happiness: Foster a sense of happiness, inner strength, and contentment, improving your overall emotional and mental well-being.

Tippy offers customized coaching packages to address your unique needs, including one-on-one coaching, and accountability. Each package is designed to facilitate your personal and spiritual development while delivering tangible benefits that can transform your life.

Schedule your complimentary initial consultation at: TippyFelzenstein.com

Complimentary Audiobook

Thank you for choosing *The 5 Day Job Search: Proven Strategies to Answering Tough Interview Questions & Getting Multiple Job Offers*. To express my gratitude, I'd like to offer you a unique opportunity: access to the complimentary audiobook, narrated personally by me, to enrich your learning experience.

Whether during your commute, at the gym, or unwinding at home, this audiobook allows you to absorb the content flexibly.

Usually priced at $20.99, I'm giving it to you for free as a token of my appreciation. Head over to annieyangfinancial.com/job-audiobook now to claim your copy. Let's continue this journey together, and here's to landing those multiple job offers!

The Gateway Affirmation

"I am more than my physical body. Because I am more than physical matter, I can perceive that which is greater than the physical world.

Therefore, I deeply desire to: to expand, to experience, to know, to understand, to control, and to use such greater energies and energy systems as may be beneficial and constructive to me and to those who follow me.

Also, I deeply desire the help and cooperation, the assistance, the understanding of those individuals whose wisdom, development and experience are equal or greater than my own.

I ask for their guidance and protection from any influence or any source that might provide me with less than my stated desires."

— *Robert A. Monroe*

Introduction

Bamboo, the fastest-growing plant on earth, takes five years to grow. It requires watering and fertilization, and throughout this time, nothing seems to happen. After five years, the bamboo suddenly breaks through the ground and grows 90 feet tall in just five weeks.

So, did the bamboo grow 90 feet in five years or five weeks?

Landing job offers in five days is akin to growing bamboo. It takes five years to nurture your seed before reaching the point of securing job offers in five days. Every overnight success was a decade in the making.

If you're the type of person who can commit to an action plan without seeing visible results for potentially years, then you possess what it takes to follow the strategies I've outlined in this book.

How can you tell if that's you?

It's straightforward. If you recognize yourself in the following mindsets, it's likely you'll remain motivated and progress toward your goals, regardless of setbacks.

This book is right for you if you're willing to do whatever it takes to have an extraordinary career—not just a good one—an extraordinary career in which you earn lots of money doing what you love. Individuals motivated primarily by money do not end up with extraordinary careers. Money can only incentivize us up to a certain point. Once our financial needs are met, we become complacent. We stop pursuing further because additional work seems to offer marginal benefit. People who truly succeed cannot imagine doing anything else with their lives. We must pursue a career we love. We must refuse to compromise or quit until we succeed.

This book is right for you if you aspire to become a leader in your field. You'll instinctively know whether that's the case. God provides us with visions of what the future could be and plants in our hearts the desire to serve humanity. We often experience a strong calling to do something and feel we must answer the call, *or else*. He has given every single one of us certain gifts. They are called gifts for a reason: we must share our gifts with others. It is in serving others that God provides us unbelievable opportunities. In an already crowded world, our gifts will make room for us. If you're unsure of your divine calling, I encourage you to download the Finding Your Calling: A Career Self-Discovery Worksheet at annieyangfinancial.com/calling. It's designed to guide you in unveiling your unique gifts and potential career path.

If you haven't discovered your calling yet, that's fine. This book is still right for you. If you constantly feel as if you've forgotten something crucial, this book is for you. When I was still discovering my calling, I experienced that feeling constantly—as if I had lost something essential. It nagged at me, and I couldn't rest until I found it. I tried numerous personality and career aptitude tests, read various books, and enrolled in courses claiming to help me find my passion. None of them worked. My calling was already within me; I merely needed to peel it layer by layer to discover its core. Once I found it, I had to accept and embrace it.

Lastly, this book is right for you if you're ready for everything in your life to change. Each year will look entirely different from the previous one. The reality is, not everyone can handle such changes, even if they are positive. I underwent at least one major transformation annually, be it leaving a toxic relationship, getting a new job, enrolling in a new course, getting married, moving to a different city, or buying a new home. My life changed so often and so dramatically that I faced several identity crises. *Who is Annie Yang?* Just as I thought I had defined myself by my job, residence, or relationship with someone else, everything would change again, and I was on the verge of breaking. I couldn't create an identity based on my ever-changing circumstances.

Who you are today is not who you will be tomorrow. You possess the power to change! We are not defined by our circumstances. It doesn't matter where you started in life. There are countless stories of people who went from rags to riches, and stories of people born with a silver spoon in their mouths who lost it all.

It only matters where you're heading. It's crucial to have a crystal clear answer to the question, "What do you want to do?" Many people can answer the question with what they don't want. There could be a million things you *don't* want. You need to answer this question with the things you *do* want. It needs to be so clear and visible in your mind that you feel as though you're already living that future in the present moment.

It doesn't matter where you are now. It doesn't matter your age either. Often, people cite "being too old" as a seemingly valid excuse for why they aren't capable of success. When we're young, we think we're not old enough. When we're older, we believe we're not young enough. In reality, the best time to start is now.

I've been encouraging my husband, a tenor, to pursue opera as a career. At 35, he is older than most successful singers in the industry, who typically start before age 30. Tenors generally begin their careers in their 20s, quit at 30 if unsuccessful, and change careers. My husband uses this as the number one reason why he can't succeed. However, since those tenors quit before finding success, it's impossible to determine if one might have achieved overnight success at age 38 if they had persevered for another eight years.

Understand that everything will come to fruition in God's time—not according to the arbitrary deadline you set for when you want things to materialize. Those tenors decided the cutoff age was 30. You can't rush God. Do your absolute best in everything you undertake and then step back, allowing God to work his magic. God uses ordinary people in extraordinary ways to demonstrate and inspire within us what's possible.

Take, for instance, Ke Huy Quan, who portrayed the male lead, Waymond Wang, in *Everything Everywhere All At Once* (2022). As a child star, he appeared in *Indiana Jones* and *The Goonies* during the 1980s. With limited acting opportunities for Asians in the 1990s and 2000s, Quan left acting in his 20s. He attended film school and focused on working behind the camera. Only after witnessing the tremendous success of *Crazy Rich Asians* (2018) did he feel compelled to join the action. At 50, he auditioned for *Everything Everywhere All At Once*, ultimately winning the 2023 Golden Globe Award and Academy Award for Best Supporting Actor in a Motion Picture. After a 38-year hiatus, he made an astonishing comeback. Quan's story inspired my husband to consider the possibilities if he pursued a singing career in his 30s. Living small impacts no one; we must chase our dreams. When ordinary people achieve success, it prompts others to question their own potential.

I experience the same struggles as everyone else. I started learning piano at 26—my parents never allowed me to take lessons as a child—and for a long time, I looked for names of professional pianists who began learning in their 20s. I couldn't find any. I was looking for the answer on the outside and realized I would have to wait and see for myself my own abilities after 10,000 hours of practice. If I couldn't find an adult example, I would have to step up and become that example. The same principle applies to you. If you can't find a role model, forge your own path and become the role model for others.

Now, let's discuss who this book isn't for:

If you look for fast and easy shortcuts or tend to fall for get-rich-quick schemes, this book isn't for you.

If you find comfort in the idea of staying in the same job for life, this book isn't for you.

If you believe trying new things is risky, this book isn't for you.

If you're unwilling to relinquish the belief that you're entitled to opportunities due to a prestigious degree, this book isn't for you.

If you've justified staying in an undesirable job due to high salaries, health insurance benefits, pensions, or work-life balance, this book isn't for you either.

If you're not prepared to dedicate a minimum of one hour per day to self-improvement, this book isn't for you.

Lastly, if you're not open to challenging the societal paradigm conditioned into you since birth, this book isn't for you.

This book may not be a right fit for eighty percent of the population. Not everyone wants my help, and I don't need to assist everyone.

I aim to help the remaining twenty percent of the population who would be receptive to the ideas presented in this book. Even then, not everyone will act on the information. Why? I spent years contemplating the answer and realized that it was counterproductive to expend energy trying to figure it out. I've come to accept that many people are *interested* in the idea of achieving success but don't genuinely want it for themselves. They wish for success to be handed to them on a silver platter, reaping the benefits without paying the price. The price isn't money; it's time and energy.

I once believed that if financially struggling individuals had access to the right information and personalized assistance, they could break the cycle of living paycheck to paycheck. Assuming they couldn't afford personalized financial advice, I offered free one-on-one help, no strings attached. I wanted to hold people accountable and help them in developing good financial habits by calling them every night for five-minute check-ins, ensuring they tracked their daily expenses. I genuinely cared about them.

While many people were drawn to the prospect of paying their bills on time, becoming debt-free, and having money saved up, they would often vanish by the third-day check-in. Despite numerous calls for several days, they never responded. I couldn't comprehend why.

One man claimed he was desperate to straighten out his finances and was "willing to do anything." We agreed to meet at his apartment on a Sunday at 6:00 pm for our first session. I confirmed with him three times that I was going to meet him on Sunday at 6:00 pm. Three times, he confirmed, "Yes." I showed up and found myself in the middle of his brother's birthday party! After waiting for 30 minutes, I asked when our financial coaching session would start. It turned out he hadn't even collected his bank and credit card statements for me to review and create a plan.

Don't people want to have lots of money and never worry about money again?

That's what they say.

The fact is, they don't.

Don't mistake interest for commitment.

Approximately five percent of readers will apply the knowledge from this book, but only partially. A mere one percent will fully commit to the action plan, going all the way, and become highly successful.

For those willing to commit, the first part of this book, *Possibility*, will be crucial in your journey. In the first part, *Possibility*, I discuss the importance of adopting the right mindset. By sharing my experiences and insights, I aim to help you establish a solid foundation for success. I will cover topics such as strategy, intuition, declaration, determination, courage, faith, and more. These traits will transform you into a highly sought-after job candidate, making employers eager to hire you, even without the conventional qualifications or experience. In fact, companies will compete to recruit you before their rivals do.

In the second part, *Preparation*, you will learn how to develop yourself to the point of securing a job offer within five days. From building your personal brand, crafting a professional email signature, optimizing your LinkedIn profile, and getting a professional headshot, I will cover everything needed to impress potential employers.

Lastly, in the third part, *Opportunity*, we explore the art of applying for jobs. I will provide practical tips on crafting a winning resume, preparing for interviews, acing interviews, and dealing with rejection. With the average career spanning fifty years, long-term thinking and planning are crucial for a rewarding journey. When you receive multiple job offers—which you undoubtedly will—you'll have the wisdom and discernment to know which opportunity to accept in order to make your big dreams a reality.

If you've determined that this book is right for you, commit fully. My advice works. I'm not asking you to do anything I haven't tried and done myself. The problem is not my advice. The problem lies in people reading books without applying the knowledge. Reading alone is not enough; you must read and apply, and then read more and apply. Don't claim you've "tried everything" when, in reality, you've only attempted a few ideas. I've never met someone who said they tried 1,000 different things like Thomas Edison did. You must follow my system in its entirety in order to achieve the desired results.

Now, if you're looking to achieve some rapid progress in your job search, we've got you covered. For those seeking quick wins, the advice in the following chapters will significantly expedite your job search:

- Chapter 15: Curating Your Online Narrative With Your Full Name
- Chapter 16: Creating a Lasting First Impression With a Professional Headshot
- Chapter 18: Optimizing Your LinkedIn Profile to Maximize Interview Requests
- Chapter 22: Expanding Your Network With a Professional Email Signature
- Chapter 25: Presenting Your Best Self in Every Situation
- Chapter 26: Enhancing Virtual Meetings With Realistic and Stylish Zoom Backgrounds
- Chapter 42: Crafting Attention-Grabbing Resumes That Reach Hiring Managers
- Chapter 43: Boosting Your Interview Chances by Applying to 50 Jobs Daily

- Chapter 44: Researching Companies to Tailor Your Interview Strategy
- Chapter 45: Mastering Fearless Salary Negotiation for the Best Offer
- Chapter 46: Harnessing Personal Power to Boost Interview Performance
- Chapter 47: Projecting Confidence to Increase Interview Success Rates
- Chapter 48: Evaluating Job Offers Beyond the Salary

Now, let's shift our focus to those who are committed to a more strategic approach. For those willing to play the long game, be prepared for an incredible journey. This book covers everything I've learned over the past decade. The content is comprehensive and thorough, spanning 49 chapters. It took me five years to reach the point of landing a job offer in less than a week, and another five years to consistently replicate this result. Fortunately, you can achieve the same results in just three years by following this system, which I had to develop through trial and error.

My progress was slow due to my low income, making it difficult to afford online courses and professional coaches. I had to save consistently for months. Then when I finally had the money, I was too scared to spend it! It was a real challenge for me to overcome the fear of spending my hard-earned money on information that might not work. Thankfully, this book is accessible even to low-income earners.

Though the plans outlined in this book may seem overwhelming, you can tackle this step by step. After all, the fastest way to eat an elephant is one bite at a time. Aim to consistently take two action steps per month. Some steps might take an hour, while others may require weeks. By being consistent, you'll average 24 action steps per year, and in five years, you'll be amazed at your progress.

To adhere to this plan, restructure your life around your goals. Evaluate your current obligations and commitments, dropping those that don't align with your objectives. Set aside two hours each day to implement the strategies in this book, ensuring no other commitments interfere.

Consider my current dedication to learning piano as an adult beginner: I restructured my life around this commitment to pave the way for my success. I don't allow clients to schedule meetings with me on Thursdays, ensuring my piano teacher has the entire day available if she needs to reschedule the lesson for earlier or later in the day. Additionally, I refrain from answering work calls and emails, helping me stay relaxed and focused for my lessons. I carefully plan all my travels around my Thursday piano lessons and attend piano performance seminars at the New England Conservatory every Friday. To further my progress, I practice piano for two hours daily and maintain a time diary to hold myself accountable.

This level of dedication serves as an example of what is required to land a job offer in five days. I have applied the same level of dedication toward advancing my career for years. Most readers will realize the amount of work involved and decide it's not worth it. However, for the one percent who believe it's worth the effort, I assure you it will be life-changing.

Part 1

Possibility

Chapter 1

Developing a Winning Strategy for Consistent Success

Is it possible to land a job offer in five days?

I mentioned to a high school classmate that I was writing a book on how to land a job offer in five days, and he initially said it wasn't possible. "But why?" I asked, "I did it three times in a row." The next day, he reconsidered and retracted his statement, concluding, "It is possible."

Whenever you think something is impossible, examine that thought. Where did it come from, and why do you believe it? If someone has already accomplished what you want to achieve, it means it's possible. I did it, so there's no reason you can't do the same with the right strategy in place.

I'm currently learning piano. My teacher assigns a piece to learn for homework. I practice a difficult section repeatedly for hours before our next lesson. Despite all the practice, I make minimal progress and keep making the same mistakes in the same spots. It's incredibly frustrating.

I go back to my lesson, telling my teacher it's impossible for me to learn piano because I try so hard without getting the results I want. She observes how I've been playing and makes a slight correction, whether by shifting the weight of my hand a certain way or moving one of my fingers to a new position. She then asks me to try again. In just five minutes, I can play the difficult section with ease.

I've experienced this scenario with my teacher multiple times. Every single time I tell her it's not possible, she proves me wrong. It's clear that my struggle was due to following the wrong strategy. When I go back home and practice with the new strategy, I don't even need to practice for long to solidify the movements into my muscle memory.

Landing a job offer in five days is like learning piano. If you follow the right strategy, you should be able to achieve this result with ease.

Chapter 2

Overcoming Obstacles With Determination and Resilience

My husband and I moved to Boston in 2018. We were coming from Lubbock, TX, a college town that had few career opportunities in anything finance related. This was the kind of town where you had to know someone who knew someone to get a job. Many companies didn't advertise their openings online.

Since I didn't know anyone, I walked into all eight banks in Lubbock with my resume in hand, but only one of them was hiring. The employees at the banks stayed over 10 years so the turnover was low. Prosperity Bank was hiring and I met 7 out of the 8 qualifications, but I got rejected within 24 hours of applying. The bank manager, Jacob Tate, told me I was unqualified for the job. I walked into a Prosperity Bank branch to verify that fact. I asked all the Prosperity Bank tellers how many of the qualifications they met when they applied and all of them told me they met only half the qualifications. Lubbock was extremely white. I blamed my rejection on the fact that I'm Asian and they probably thought I didn't speak fluent English based on looking at my last name.

I ended up working at Domino's Pizza for a year and a half. During my time in Lubbock, I worked five part-time jobs all at once, plus a few odd jobs, just to make enough money. I never took a day off. I wasn't confident I could get a job in Boston that wasn't Domino's Pizza. When I moved, I packed my Domino's

Pizza hat and T-shirt just in case I ended up working at Domino's Pizza (sad, I know).

I wanted to make money. I was sick and tired of working my butt off, trying to convince everyone that I was smart, capable, and hardworking, but no one ever wanted to give me the opportunity to prove myself. My whole life, people underestimated me. With a new beginning about to start in Boston, this was finally my chance.

I had only five years to make a name and reputation for myself in Boston because my husband and I might not have stayed after he finished his PhD. It was important for me to establish a solid career within these five years so I could convince my husband to settle down in Boston for good. I hate moving cities because every time you move, you need to re-establish your network and build up your reputation again from scratch.

I was determined to get a job. I applied for 50 jobs a day until I received a job offer. I started applying on a Saturday. On Monday, I already had several companies reach out to me for an interview. One of them interviewed me that Friday and said, "I like your hustle. You have spunk. I never see that in people." The next day, he emailed me a job offer, which I accepted. I landed the job in seven days. I was so grateful that God had listened and given me what I wanted.

The new job didn't turn out to be what I thought. My new boss was a crazy micromanager who timed my bathroom breaks. He gave us a 15-minute break at 10:00am. One day, I left for break at 10:01am, so I returned at 10:16am, and he yelled at me for stealing one minute of paid work time.

There were a bunch of other problems. But mainly, he didn't allow me to enter the one-inch stack of paper bills into Quick-Books for processing without his permission. Every day, a new fire had to be put out when a bill came due and there wasn't enough money to pay it. It didn't seem normal. So, I added up all the bills manually on a calculator and compared it to the company's bank balance. I realized the company was operating in the red. He owed over $100,000.00 more in the next 30 days than he had available cash in the bank. I looked at his bank register—he had bounced one employee's paycheck earlier that year. It was like living paycheck to paycheck, but on a company-wide scale. I wanted job security. I didn't want any of my own paychecks to bounce. It was time to look for another job.

I started applying for jobs on my phone on a Tuesday morning while taking the train to work. To my surprise, after work that Tuesday, I got a request for an interview scheduled the following Monday. Two company partners interviewed me. The first partner asked where I was from and I said, "Brooklyn." It turned out he also grew up in Brooklyn and he jokingly said, "You're hired." The second partner asked why I was looking for a new job and I said I didn't want to be micromanaged. "You're hired," he said.

Did I really just land a job offer in only six days? I got lucky twice?

Chapter 3

Setting Clear Goals: Secure a $35,000 Raise

When I started working in my new job, I created a financial plan to buy a house in exactly two years. My husband and I needed to save for the down payment and show two years' worth of continuous employment to qualify for the mortgage.

One year in, my husband and I went to several open houses to get a good idea of what we could afford to buy. Our financial plan was to buy a $300,000.00 property, but we visited houses listed at $400,000.00 as well.

My husband wouldn't stop imagining the possibility of us living together in one of those $400,000.00 houses. He fantasized the kind of happy life we could have together. I really wanted to make my husband happy.

Rerunning the numbers, I calculated we could save enough for the down payment, but we wouldn't get approved for a $400,000.00 property.

My income was only $45,000.00 and I needed to earn at least $70,000.00 to qualify. My husband couldn't earn more money because he was a full-time student, so the responsibility was 100% on me.

During the entire year I worked at that company, my coworker kept asking for a $1.00/hour raise—that's $2,080.00 a year—but his requests kept getting rejected. Everyone agreed his work was amazing, but the three partners refused his request.

I needed a $25,000.00 raise, which was exponentially more money than my coworker's request. There was no way on earth I would receive that raise. It was time to look for a new job again.

"$70,000 SALARY."

I wrote this on a piece of paper and taped it to the wall.

Declaring what you want is how you create possibilities in life. Every time I wanted to accomplish a goal, I would write it down on a piece of paper and tape it to the wall. There has never been an instance where declaring what I wanted did not work out for me. This time, I declared how much money I wanted to make, and nothing was going to stop me.

I got what I wanted because I kept all the promises I made to myself. Whenever I made a promise, no matter how small, I always followed through. If someone said, "Let's have lunch or coffee sometime," I always scheduled a time to make it happen. If I had an appointment for 4:00pm, I would show up at exactly 4:00pm, not 4:02pm. Even if the other person didn't remember asking for lunch or didn't look at the exact time I showed up, I fulfilled my end of the deal.

The most important promises you make are the promises you make to yourself. Whether it's promising yourself you'll wake up at 6:00am, you'll stick to a new diet for 90 days, or you'll read ten books this year.

No one is morally policing you to make sure you keep these promises. There is no visible or immediate consequence because these promises don't affect other people. But just because you don't see the consequences doesn't mean they don't exist. The consequence is the gradual erosion of the power of your words. Keeping your smallest promises transforms the relationship you have with yourself. Self-confidence comes from believing you are capable. And if you're not capable of following through on the smallest commitments, subconsciously, you'll question whether you can accomplish great things.

Create your promises with intention from now on. It's okay if you cannot keep your commitments, so long as you verbally communicate this to other people right away. You're allowed to change your commitments by making and following through on new promises.

After declaring the new salary I wanted, I applied for 50 jobs a day, just like last time. I didn't feel pressured to land a job offer quickly because I had an entire year to sort it out. I started applying on Monday evening. The next morning, I checked my emails in bed right after waking up. To my surprise, one company had requested an interview for that Thursday.

On Tuesday and Wednesday, I was getting phone calls and emails nonstop from recruiters, and I even did a phone interview with a tech start up. There was one particular recruiter, Van, who asked me what salary I was looking for. I told him I needed $70,000.00 a year.

Based on his 10 years of experience in recruiting for accounting positions, he told me since I didn't have an accounting degree listed on my resume, the most money I could ever make in this field was $55,000.00 - $60,000.00, "*If you're lucky.*" He told me about the $55,000.00 opportunities I was qualified for.

I was so mad. I told Van I worked harder than any goddamn accounting employee who graduated with an accounting degree. I learned faster on the job than all of them. At every single job I've worked, I outworked every single person. Even going back to my very first job at 18 years old, 100% of my bosses always begged me again and again to stay whenever I gave notice of resignation (the only exception was that guy who timed my bathroom break). I told him that in my experience, work ethic was far more valuable to employers than a piece of paper.

Van relented and said he'll push my resume through for the $70,000.00 job opportunity and get back to me. The next day, he called to say the company wasn't interested and to trust that he was right. "You aren't capable of making more than $55,000.00 a year because of your lack of formal accounting credentials." The more he rubbed it in my face, the more I wanted to prove him wrong.

33

I went to the interview on Thursday and my future boss was super impressed by me. Three times during the interview, he asked how much money I wanted so that he could craft an offer. I refused to give a number. I kept saying repeatedly, "I want to get paid the salary equivalent to how much value you believe I bring to your company." He changed the question and asked me how much money I would need to qualify for the mortgage. I said, "$70,000.00, but don't assume that I'm going to accept your offer. I'm going to go back to my current employer and ask for a match, and if they match, I'm going to turn down your offer."

"No problem with me, Annie."

The next day, my future boss offered me $80,000.00. It was a new personal record—a written job offer in five days. Three times in a row, I knew it was no longer luck—it was skill!

I emailed Van to tell him he was wrong.

Then I went back to the three partners at my current job and explained, "I needed to make more money so that I could qualify for a mortgage. I already have a job offer for $80,000.00 but if you could match it, then I'll stay because I really love this company like family with all my heart."

The three partners asked me to leave the room and huddled for ten minutes arguing with each other. Finally, they called me back in the room and said the very best they could offer was $70,000.00. I was shocked by their offer. They were willing to give me a $25,000.00 raise. At the same time, I was so heartbroken because it was hard for me to leave $10,000.00 on the table. I took the new job.

Chapter 4

Empowering Yourself When Others Disapprove

My new boss was wonderful. He hired me because he recognized my talents and wanted me to create systems and processes for his company. I loved him a lot. He always treated me with a lot of kindness and respect. It was almost like he viewed me more like an equal peer or a partner, rather than an employee. Every time I had a new idea to help run his company more efficiently, he gave me the green light. My coworkers undermined me every step of the way, but it didn't matter because my boss's word was final.

One day, my boss said, "Annie, wouldn't it be a great idea if we put an FAQ on the website? Our administrative assistant is spending too much time answering frequently asked questions on the phone. She could spend the time doing more productive tasks instead." I agreed and told him I would reach out to her the next day about jotting down the questions she frequently got on the phone calls, and we would come up with the answers together.

The next day, I asked the administrative assistant to jot down the questions after every phone call. I didn't get the response I expected. Apparently, I made her feel threatened. She complained to my boss that I was "coming after her job." My boss, not sure what to do, quickly pinned the blame on me. He said that his idea yesterday was only meant to be shared with me, and that he never intended to implement it.

I didn't like that. I can tolerate being undermined at work, but I draw the line at being prevented from working on brand new projects. That's the only way to gain new skills and experiences.

Should I apply for new jobs again? I could easily get a new job by the end of the week, but I figured every company would have someone on the team who might feel threatened and create unnecessary drama.

I formed my own company, Annie Yang Financial Corporation, after weighing various options.

I'm the boss now, so I don't need to ask anyone for permission.

So often, we wait for an authority figure to give us permission to do amazing things. No one wants to give you permission. Everyone just wants you to have a mediocre life. If people gave you permission to chase your wildest dreams, they would spiral into an identity crisis. When you go after your dreams, you cause people to question why they're not going after their own dreams. Facing this truth is too uncomfortable. The only person who can give you permission is yourself.

I still work the same full-time job while growing my company. I have zero fear of losing my job. I was fully transparent with my boss and asked that he give me enough flexibility to make it happen. I told my boss I wasn't sure how long it would take me to make the company profitable enough to quit my job and run my business full-time, but when the time came, I would give two months' notice and train my replacement. I would even write a detailed training manual.

He agreed to the plan, but the next month, I saw a ZipRecruiter charge on the company credit card. I'm the accountant so I see all the finances. As far as I was aware, we weren't hiring anyone new. I logged into the ZipRecruiter account and saw that my boss had put a job listing to replace me. I didn't say anything.

A few weeks later, he told me he secretly tried to replace me but couldn't find anyone in the market that had the same talents and skills to do the job extremely well. It scared him I would suddenly walk out on him one day when the time finally came. I kept reassuring him he could trust me. We are on very good terms today.

Chapter 5

Attracting Multiple Job Offers Effortlessly

After I created Annie Yang Financial Corporation, even though I didn't proactively apply for jobs, three companies reached out to me wanting to create a job just for me. Since I no longer plan to work another job, I'm unable to share more stories of landing a job offer in five days, but I can share some interesting anecdotes about the different opportunities that have opened up for me.

The first offer I received was from a vice president of a bank who heard about my skills and reputation and wanted me to join his team. They weren't necessarily hiring—they were willing to create a brand-new position just for my talents and abilities. This was mind-boggling because only four years earlier, Prosperity Bank told me I was unqualified for an entry-level job. I turned this bank down.

The second offer was from a real estate developer that I was marketing to for Annie Yang Financial Corporation. He asked me for my background, and after I explained, he offered me a full-time job asking me to just forget about building my company and work for him instead. Again, creating a brand-new position just for me. He asked me many times how much money would it take to poach me away from my current full-time job? I told him that no amount of money could get me to quit my current job because my boss gave me so much flexibility. I work only 20-25 hours a week, but I get paid the same full-time salary. I don't think any company can offer me a deal this attractive.

The third offer was a weird one. I had a client I was trying to dismiss. The client wasn't following instructions, so I told him we're just not a good fit and I gave him a 30-day notice of termination. On the 29th day, I got a phone call from the owner of my biggest competitor. He said he was calling to introduce himself.

I said, "I already know exactly who you are. I researched all my competitors. What do you want?"

He said, "Your client called me because he was shopping around for a new service provider. I just wanted to find out the future goal of Annie Yang Financial Corporation. Is this something you're just doing on the side to make some extra money? I watched your YouTube video about not getting along with your coworkers. Are you doing Annie Yang Financial Corporation just so you can quit your current job?"

I told him, "Annie Yang Financial Corporation is going to be a billion-dollar company. I'm going to make enough profit at this company to quit my job. In a few years, I'm going to eat your lunch. I'm going to put you out of business. I'm very much serious. Tell me the truth. Why are you calling me?"

He kept dodging my question. Instead, he said, "I really liked your social media presence and I wish there was someone like you at my company to run things more efficiently. My team isn't the kind that enjoys looking for better ways to do things." It didn't make any sense. He wasn't answering the question about what exactly he hoped to get from calling me, his competitor. The conversation finally ended after an hour.

A few days later, my client told me he wanted to stay with me and agreed to follow my instructions. I asked the client what on earth happened in his sales call with my competitor that led the owner himself to call me?

My competitor had 100 people working for him, so it was a shock that I got on the owner's radar, especially since my company was so small. My client told me that the salesperson had never seen an accounting system like this before and wanted to show the owner. When the owner looked at my work, he said it was 100% perfect and that my advice was spot on. My client said the owner was excited and really wanted to offer me a job right after the sales call was over. But after the owner heard me talk about my plans to eat his lunch, he backtracked.

Chapter 6

Being in High Demand for Ultimate Financial Security

I have a lot of financial security in a different way. I always saved a lot of my money because I felt scared that I would lose my job. Despite how much I saved, I never truly felt secure. Currently, I haven't saved enough money to be financially independent. Far from it, because most of my money gets reinvested back into growing my company.

Now I feel different. The best way I can describe it is, I feel really rich inside. I know my skills are in high demand, that I can easily land a new full-time job in five days repeatedly. I actually take more calculated risks in my career now that I wouldn't have taken before. It's comforting to know that even if a company wasn't hiring, they would open a new opportunity just for me by creating a job catered to my specific skill set. They can immediately see the value I would bring.

Most people have the illusion of job security. They feel secure in knowing they have a steady paycheck. They know exactly how much they will get paid and when.

But that feeling you get from a steady paycheck is not actual security. As I've explained, a company can live paycheck to paycheck just like an individual and bounce your paycheck. A company can also spend so much money that it can no longer meet its debt obligations and needs an injection of outside capital to keep operating. Another company can acquire the company.

Then the parent company can decide to cease operations at any moment. A company might decide to please its shareholders by laying off its workforce to show a profitable annual report. You cannot control what a company does.

For actual security, you need to be in such high demand that you can easily land a new job and avoid affecting your cash flow. The other option is to own a business and have multiple sources of income—all your customers would have to fire you at the same time before you can go out of business.

Chapter 7

Unlocking Your Unlimited Potential

"I am more than my physical body because I am more than physical matter. I can perceive that which is greater than the physical world."

— *Robert A. Monroe*

At age 15, I had a profound experience that forever changed the direction of my life.

My ex-boyfriend put his hand out before me. He said, "Imagine a ball on my hand. You can do anything with the ball."

In my mind's eye, I imagined the ball bouncing up and down on the palm of his hand, then rolling around in a circle clockwise, and finally rolling back and forth between the palm of his hand and his elbow. He described what he felt: "I felt a heavy weight on my hand in a pulsating rhythm, then it went around in a circle, and then I felt the weight traveling up and down my arm."

He held my hand and asked me to think about a number between one and nine for an entire minute. I thought of the number seven intently and after one minute, he said, "Seven." We did this three times, and he stated the correct number each time.

I didn't understand what was happening. He explained that there is more to the physical reality that we see around us. There is an entire spiritual realm that exists beyond our five senses.

He said, "Everything we physically see was first created in our minds. It takes a long time for things to manifest from the spiritual plane to the physical plane, but you instantly create whatever you're creating in your mind as energy. The ball on my hand that you imagined in your mind was energy and you know it's real because I felt it and could describe accurately what you did.

"I've been practicing a series of meditation tapes called *The Gateway Experience* by the Monroe Institute. You expressed you don't want to go to college. You're choosing a hard path. If you want to be successful, learn to manipulate your energy to manifest all your dreams into reality. I put *The Gateway Experience* meditations on this USB flash drive. Practice the exercises every night before you go to sleep. Do this for several months and then you'll be able to control your energy."

There were 36 meditation exercises total, and I did each for one week before moving on to the next exercise. I wanted to make sure I mastered the technique because I sometimes fell asleep.

My perspective on life changed. Prior to that, I felt like I was constantly fighting the limits that well-meaning adults placed on me. Something within me shifted. In an advanced exercise, I reached such a deep and relaxed state of consciousness, I felt like the confines of my physical body no longer existed. It felt as if my soul, the core essence of who I am, expanded and combined with the surrounding space, as if I was one with the space, the universe. My entire life I never belonged, like I never fit in anywhere. For the first time, I felt peace arriving back home.

I experimented with energy. My ex-boyfriend owned a pet parrot named Sonny and he wouldn't allow me to feed Sonny peanuts out of fear that he would get fat. I imagined opening the jar of peanuts and feeding Sonny a couple of peanuts. Within a few seconds, Sonny would start chewing as if he was eating peanuts for real. It was cute because it looked like he was eating the air.

When a dog didn't stop barking, I sent it loving energy and wrapped it in a blanket of white light. Within a few seconds, it calmed down. On the train, whenever I saw someone looking unhappy, I did the same thing and within a few seconds, that person's facial expression would change to be more at peace.

Whenever I walked alone at night, I would wrap myself inside an energy balloon for protection. One night, I was only two blocks away from home and I suddenly felt an urge to jog instead of walk, so I jogged. I passed by a man who asked, "Excuse me, what time is it?" Instead of taking out my phone, I kept jogging and told him, "It's around 10:15pm." After I got home, I realized I had avoided getting mugged. It was strange to ask for the time since cell phones were already commonplace.

I started having dreams where I would leave my body. Sometimes I had dreams flying through the air. In one particular dream, I was in a vast, expansive room with a gigantic globe of light. I flew around the light. As I settled on the ground, several spirits came to me and told me they were spirit guides helping me in my current life. I felt deep serenity that I haven't been able to replicate since.

In another dream, I met two more spirit guides that took the form of beautiful-looking women. We were inside a fancy hotel. I asked them, "Who am I? Why was I born? And what am I here to do?" I felt like there was something I had promised to do, but I had forgotten what it was. The spirits said they knew the answer, but they weren't allowed to give it to me and that rediscovering it was part of my journey.

Soon after, I learned a lesson to be careful with my words. I realized our words create our reality. One time, my phone's battery was at 3% and the last text message I sent my friend was, "My phone's battery is about to die." After my phone shut down, I charged it, but it never turned back on. The battery really died, and I had to buy a new phone. "My battery is about to die" is something people commonly say. I didn't grasp the power of my words back then. I now know in the future to say, "My phone is low on battery," instead.

Over the past decade, the time it took to manifest something kept getting shorter. I would think about what I want, and then I'm coincidentally placed in the situation where I meet the right person at the right time and the right place, and it eventually leads to my desired result.

On my 21st birthday, I wished to meet my life partner and get married. I had big dreams, so I wanted a man by my side, supporting me emotionally and mentally while I worked through my life challenges. I told everyone I knew that I wanted this and that if they knew someone single, to make the introduction so we can go on a date.

Five weeks later, I temporarily moved back in with my parents. I committed to focusing all my energy on finishing my bachelor's degree in only two years instead of four, and living with my parents would save me time by not having to cook. Since I no longer needed my mattress, I listed it for sale on Craigslist on a Sunday night. I got an inquiry from only one man, and he wanted to pick up the mattress on Wednesday evening. I didn't want to wait until Wednesday and evenings weren't a good time for me either. I wanted the mattress gone as soon as possible, but since he was the only one who contacted me, I agreed to sell it to him.

When the man came to get the mattress, I couldn't help but stare at him. *I've seen him somewhere before, but where?* His name, Handrio, was too unique, and he'd just moved to Brooklyn. He was new in town, which was the reason he was buying a mattress in the first place. I couldn't pinpoint why he looked so familiar. I looked closely at his face many times to confirm that we had never met before. I thought it through again and again. I concluded it was definitely my first time meeting him in this life.

Within an hour after he picked up the mattress, at least five people texted me asking if the mattress was still available. It was strange because the listing had been up for three days and no one had asked about it in that time period. But right after I sold it, people were asking?

48

The man texted me the next day about how comfortable the mattress was. He remembered that I had been carrying a black case yesterday, but he mistook it for a violin case (it was a photography lighting kit) and asked if I was a musician. We continued the conversation from there.

We went on a first date. After the date, every morning the first thing I heard after I woke up was the soft and sweet voice of a woman that said some variation of, "He's the one you're going to marry," "You're going to marry him," or "He's the guy." This happened every morning for several weeks straight.

I proposed four months into our relationship, and he turned my proposal down. I thought the voice lied to me. Four months after Handrio rejected my proposal, he backtracked and asked if we could get married. We got married one month before my 22nd birthday, just in time for my 21st birthday wish to come true. The voice turned out to be right.

In hindsight, an invisible hand was shielding me from all the potential mattress buyers contacting me. I can't think of any other logical explanation. This story could be a Hollywood movie.

I have met so many people through pure coincidence, finding out later that they happened to be the right person to help me with the problem I was experiencing. For example, I didn't know how to drive and couldn't afford formal driving lessons. It was affecting my ability to apply for jobs because I had no way to get to work! I was walking on my husband's campus and a man approached me and started hitting on me. I said, "I'm married but I'd be happy to be friends." We became friends and I later found out he used to be a commercial truck driver, delivering goods all across the United States on an 18-wheeler. I didn't ask him to teach me to drive—he offered, and all he wanted from me was $5.00 tacos from Taco Bell.

I've gotten to the point now where I would think about something in my mind, and within 24 hours, someone related to what I was thinking about would contact me randomly.

A few years ago, I was thinking about who I wanted to help with their finances. Who was my ideal customer? I played around with the thought of helping newlywed couples set a strong financial foundation because the #1 cause of divorce is money fights. The next day, a newly married couple coincidentally reached out to me asking me for financial advice. I decided this wasn't my ideal customer, but merely thinking about this idea attracted these people into my life.

Just a few months ago, I walked past a buffet and thought about an acquaintance I had lunch with at that buffet. We hadn't spoken in months, but within three hours of me replaying the memory in my head, he texted me out of the blue saying he wanted to get lunch together at that buffet again.

Fairly recently, I realized throughout the past decade, I've been hearing voices in my head that communicate what my next moves should be. I always assumed they were my own thoughts. When I asked other people if they had the same chatter and conversations in their head, they told me no. I realized the voices were not mine and were totally separate from me as an individual. I know this because they told me to write this book at 1:00am. I tried negotiating, asking them to come back in the morning because I wanted to sleep. But the voices said no and just kept feeding me the information for this book until I finally got up and obeyed their request.

There is more to life than meets the eye. We get bogged down by the physical realm because, as adults, we have to get a job to earn money and pay our bills. Plenty of jobs out there consume over 40 hours a week because of a culture of working overtime. Even if you work less than 40 hours, the job could be physically, mentally, and emotionally draining to the point where you no longer have energy remaining to truly think, explore, and question whether there is more to life.

Who are you? Are you your name? Your personality? Your body? Your job? We are none of those things. Each of us has a core essence—a soul. We are souls living in human bodies. To tap into our limitless potential and create the life of our dreams, we must first know and remember who we really are.

Chapter 8

Accessing Your Inner Wisdom
for Career Guidance

Wisdom is already within. When we want something and we're blocked because we don't know how to get there, we look for the answer outside of ourselves. You already have the answer. Your body is trying to communicate with you but you're not listening. We ignore those warning signs, believing everything is going perfectly fine, when in reality, we're headed toward disaster. And it isn't until the day we get diagnosed with a disease that we hear the wake-up call. Disease is really dis-ease which starts in the mind and the spirit.

One big reason we find it difficult to tune into our body and what it is trying to tell us is because we numb our feelings with substances. Being in our bodies can feel uncomfortable. Panic, anxiety, depression, fear, confusion, horror, embarrassment, despair, doubt, anger, and worry—all these feelings create physical sensations in our body that hurt. Instead of feeling these sensations, breathing into the pain and reminding ourselves that the feelings hurt but can't harm us, we dilute and numb the sensations with substances. Addictive substances such as drugs, tobacco, alcohol, processed foods, and sugar all block our ability to feel. Unfortunately, we can't block only the negative. When we block our feelings in this manner, we block our intuition as well, which causes us to make the wrong decisions.

I felt depressed watching all my friends from high school go off to highly prestigious universities while I stayed back and worked minimum wage jobs. They posted photos every week of the new friends they made and the parties they attended. I felt left out. I felt like I was falling behind and became depressed. I didn't want to face my feelings and I didn't want to be settled in my body. I wanted to die and just end it all.

I numbed the pain by eating three bars of chocolate every day. I would feel happy for 30 minutes after eating chocolate but then my head would start hurting. I would feel dizzy and always end up crashing into my bed for the rest of the day. The pain caused by the sugar served as a distraction to avoid dealing with my real problems.

No outsider could tell I had developed this addiction, because I exercised a lot and was skinny. But my doctor ran a blood test, and my sugar levels were so high, she declared me borderline pre-diabetic at age 19. I felt so guilty when my doctor said she knew I had a sweet tooth. When my dad opened my bedroom door without my permission, he found a mountain full of candy wrappers next to my bed, and I felt ten times worse.

I knew I had to stop. I practiced *The Gateway Experience* meditation exercises every night, just like years earlier. Through those exercises, I learned to settle back into my body and be at peace with where I was in life. The chocolate addiction naturally went away on its own after a month of meditation practice. I never felt the urge to eat chocolate again. One year later, I tested for a bunch of allergies. I'm allergic to chocolate. Isn't that ironic? I think my body decided, "No more chocolate. Period."

To reconnect with your intuition, be willing to feel all the sensations in your body, both good and bad. Stop feeding your body addictive substances. Meditate and clean up your diet. Ask yourself, in one word, what is the feeling you're experiencing? Then, where is the physical pain in your body? Describe the physical pain like you're trying to explain it to an alien who has never experienced pain before.

Feelings hurt, but they cannot harm. Have the courage to feel the entire spectrum from happiness to sadness in its fullest intensity. Be honest with yourself and face your emotions. This is all part of the human experience. After practicing this way of life, the intuition will become as clear as daylight. Listen to your body.

Chapter 9

Cultivating Courage to Face Your Fears

Carving our own path in life, a path totally different from the traditional route of graduating from college, working a steady, secure job, and then retiring at 65, never feels good.

No one ever tells you this:

Courage feels terrible.

We admire courageous people like they are heroes. We hold them in high regard. We develop a false picture in our minds that courage should feel good. Courage has never felt good and never will.

What is courage? Anytime we want to do something new, we feel scared. Courage is the act of committing yourself to doing it anyway, despite the fear. We confuse courage with confidence. We feel confident when we do something we're already good at. Confidence stems from having results you can point to and use as validation.

When you're doing something new, of course you're not good at it yet, so the feeling you get is courage, not confidence. When I feel courage, my chest tightens up, my breathing turns shallow, and my shoulders roll forward because I feel small. I feel incapable of overcoming what lies before me. Despite feeling fear and doubt, I muster up courage every day. I muster up courage all the way until it finally transitions into confidence.

We don't give ourselves enough space to develop our courage. Right after we decide to try something new, we think, *but I've never done this before.* We believe that since we've never done this before, it means we'll *never* be able to do it. Our brains play tricks on us to avoid stepping into courage.

We can learn and do anything we set our minds to. There are so many things we didn't know how to do at some point in our lives, but we eventually learned how to do it and we take that for granted. Basic things, like walking, speaking, reading, feeding yourself without making a mess, tying your shoes, boiling water, turning a doorknob, baking a cake, typing, dialing a phone number. The list is endless. When we were children, everything we did was a first. We had never done it before. And we didn't care! We just kept exploring and trying different things without getting emotionally hung up.

As children, we look forward to the future. We see the future with so much potential because it doesn't matter that we never did it in the past.

As adults, we get emotionally hung up on things we've never done before, whether that's landing a job offer in five days, creating a highly successful business, becoming the first homeowner in your family, writing a bestselling book, moving to a new country, learning a new language, learning an instrument, getting married, or becoming a parent.

The emotional hang-up happens because we mistakenly look at our past to determine our future. But the past does not predict or determine the future. Just because we've never done something before, doesn't mean we're never able to do it. Those two concepts are completely distinct from each other. Don't confuse the two.

Give yourself the space to feel courage.

I've never done this before, and I'm stepping into the possibility that I can do it.

The most challenging experience where I had to develop a lot of courage was in high school. In the summer before junior year of high school, I stayed with my aunt in China for two months. For the first time in my life, I had so much time on my hands. I always went to top schools, so my teachers would overload us with so much homework that I had little time to stop and think about the important question: What do I want to be when I grow up?

I surfed the Internet a lot and I stumbled upon blogs like Zen Habits and The Minimalists. These bloggers quit their soul sucking six-figure corporate jobs and sold all their belongings in search of a more meaningful life. They were saying things completely contrary to what my schoolteachers and guidance counselors told me my whole life. Essentially, that the traditional path of going to college, getting a 9-5 job, and buying a house and car does not lead to happiness.

I'm from an immigrant community. For many immigrants, getting a 9-5 job is the definition of achieving the American dream. They never had a steady paycheck and job security, so that is their dream for their kids. That's what my parents wanted for me. To get a government job and collect a retirement pension. Because once you're hired, you'll never get fired. They never wanted me to aspire to greatness or to chase my dreams and passions. They thought dreams were meant to stay dreams.

But if Zen Habits and The Minimalists were right and adults really lived like that after high school, why go through all that trouble of going to college? To end up in a job you hate? To quit that job so you can find the one you love? Why detour? Why can't I just take the time to discover my passions first, and then pursue my dream job?

I reflected and concluded that I've been in school my entire life and didn't know enough about the real world to make a good decision. While I was academically smart, it was very possible my final interest didn't lie inside a subject covered in university. My parents were poor, so it didn't make sense to borrow tens of thousands of dollars in student loans to discover my interests, when I could do it for free at the library.

I told my friends about my plans to forego college, make money, and get my education at the library. My friends' parents told them to stay away from me because I was a bad influence. My friends also found my plans to be far-fetched and crazy, and many of them stopped talking to me. I became a social outcast.

I asked my favorite teachers for advice. Since I was an outstanding student, all of them suggested I go to college. They didn't have advice for alternative options.

Mrs. Garcia came into the picture. The school hired her as a guidance counselor during my junior year, so she was brand new. She met one-on-one with all her students to ask which colleges we were planning to apply to. When she asked me, I told her I didn't plan to go to college.

Mrs. Garcia looked at my transcript and my extracurriculars and saw that I had what it took to get into an Ivy League university. But I wasn't interested in any of that. Since her job was to give me guidance, I asked her what were my options if I didn't want to go to college? What jobs could I work with no experience? What companies could I apply to? How do I apply for a job? How do I get an apprenticeship or internship?

She didn't provide any options outside of college. Instead, we met every week for two years. She pushed the same message repeatedly:

"You're throwing your life away. Not going to college will be the biggest regret in your entire life."

She repeatedly drilled into me, "You're destined to be a failure."

One morning, Mrs. Garcia pulled me out of physics class. She didn't tell me in advance that I was walking into a special meeting involving her, my mom, my dad, as well as the director of the guidance counseling department.

Mrs. Garcia looked my mom in the eyes and said, "Your daughter will always be a failure."

She asked my parents for their thoughts about my choice, and all my dad said was, "We're not responsible for Annie after she turns 18. It's her life."

I felt so demoralized. I was about to give in. Maybe Mrs. Garcia was right after all! She was the adult in the room. Adults always knew more than kids. Adults were the ones who knew how life worked in the real world.

But as I was contemplating Mrs. Garcia possibly being right, a man's voice with the mightiness and gravity of Zeus's thunder screamed inside my head:

"Annie, if you go straight to college, you'll always regret it for the rest of your life. You're not supposed to go down that path. It's not the right path for you. Do not listen to her!"

What was that voice?

I never heard that before.

That voice wasn't mine.

Strange.

Whatever it was, the voice felt *right*.

I couldn't ignore the feeling.

What did my future have in store for me?

What was the journey I was about to embark on?

Where was it going to lead?

If going straight to college was the wrong path, did that mean there was such a thing as the right path?

If there was a right path, did that mean I had a destiny?

What about my free will?

Why did my path have to differ from everyone else's?

Why me?

I felt scared out of my mind since all the adults in my life warned that I was going the wrong way.

I'd never done this before.

Most people who didn't go straight to college had poor grades.

What happened to people who had good grades but didn't want to go to college?

61

Did the second group end up working at McDonalds the rest of their lives too?

Despite the unknowns, I gathered the courage to follow my heart.

Chapter 10

Reinventing Yourself After Hitting Rock Bottom

I have a secret I've shared with only a few people in my life:

I used to be a foot fetish model.

How on earth did I get to a point where I was on the cusp of becoming a prostitute?

Everyone today sees me as a responsible woman who always stands for her values and principles.

I wasn't always this way.

What is my calling?

I didn't know the answer.

I didn't know what exactly I was working toward.

I went in the wrong direction.

My first job right after high school at age 18 was working at a massage parlor for $120.00/week in cash. I worked 60 hours a week, so it worked out to be only $3.00/hour. If I gave a massage, I got to keep the tips, but most people tipped $10.00 - $20.00 for a massage, and I averaged only one massage in an entire workday.

I had no adult guidance. No one ever explained to me that it was illegal to be paid less than minimum wage and that my employer was skirting the law by paying me in cash. I naively believed it was a good thing to be paid under the table (in cash) because my parents were immigrants who were paranoid about the government taking all their money away just like in China in the 1950s and 1960s. Many immigrants get paid under the table, so that was all I knew. I thought it was totally normal and acceptable, and that it was actually better than doing it the legal way: reporting the income and paying income taxes.

I saved 50% of my income and after a few months, I had approximately three thousand dollars saved up. I was sick and tired of working so hard for so little pay, so I quit. Convinced that I wouldn't be able to make more than minimum wage if I didn't go to college, I felt cornered. Was this truly my destiny? To work another job that would take advantage of me the same way the massage parlor owner did?

I thought the solution was to start my own business so that no one could determine my pay.

I went on Amazon and spent $500.00 on a ton of books to learn HTML and CSS so I could design a website—not to design websites for a living, but to design a website where I could sell stuff online. I wanted to sell belly dance clothes on bellybae.com.

I diligently studied day after day. One evening, while studying at my boyfriend's place, my boyfriend got mad at me for my ability to just sit down and get work done. He wanted to be a doctor, but he didn't have a passion for medicine—he just wanted high pay and high job security. He told me it wasn't fair. He constantly needed to motivate himself, whereas I could just study hour after hour with no one to push me. Even back then, I did things simply because I wanted to. I never did things just because someone told me I needed to. When you do things out of pleasure, you need no one to push you.

I successfully designed the website. But I needed inventory. I spent $1,000.00 on belly dancing clothes through Alibaba and posted them on bellybae.com.

But I didn't know how to make any sales. How could I market and advertise and get people to know about bellybae.com?

I couldn't figure it out. I lacked the experience and financial resources. I had only $1,500.00 left in my savings and started feeling panic and anxiety. I didn't want to work another job ever again. I didn't have it in me to go through the $3.00/hour thing again.

My boyfriend had a solution. I could become a foot model at foot fetish parties. He said it was a legitimate way to make money and he had found it on Craigslist. He showed me pictures of their website and there were many photos of scantily dressed young women showing off their feet in various sexually suggestive positions.

I was desperate at this point. The thought of men touching me repulsed me. But I thought, how bad could it be? It's just my feet.

I "interviewed" with the foot fetish party owner, Jason. At the "interview," he played with my feet and licked my feet all over. In porn movies, the actors do this stupid scripted interview before getting down to business. The interview was just like that. It was as awkward as you imagine. He hired me to be a foot model.

At the first party, three men kissed, fondled, and licked my feet. They weren't supposed to go above the knee, but one of them violated that rule and I felt uncomfortable. I made $120.00 in only 30 minutes. Compared to making $120.00/week at the massage parlor, it was a lot of money. Maybe I could do this for money since it was only once in a while, I thought.

I didn't earn any money at the second party because hardly anyone showed up. It was the weekend of a major football game.

The third party was a completely different animal. I was told the dress code required women to wear a bra and thong and nothing else. I followed the dress code, but I was really uncomfortable because I felt practically naked.

There was a lot of alcohol at the party. Lots of people were smoking indoors so I had trouble breathing. The music played so loud that it was hard to hear people talking even when they were standing right next to me. Women were dry humping men on the sofa.

A man named Marcus, the same age as my father, approached me and said he wanted to play with me in the private room in the back. I said OK. No one informed me that the men could do whatever they wanted in the back room. They weren't restricted to only feet. For ten whole minutes, I felt so violated. The clock moved so slow.

I should've gone home after that, but I stayed thinking that what happened was an outlier.

A second man approached me, also my father's age. He wanted to go in the back room as well and I consented. Same thing again. Ten minutes of violating my body and my soul.

All that just to make $80.00.

I didn't lose my virginity that night, thank goodness. But I left so disgusted with myself. I had no dignity. I was now a dirty woman. The essence of my soul shattered into pieces.

I had never felt lonelier and more disconnected from society than that night taking the MTA home at 4:00am.

I couldn't fall asleep.

I called my boyfriend at 7:00am to tell him what happened. Instead of feeling sorry and supportive about what happened to me, he responded like I was dirty.

Marcus, from the party, called me a week later asking to have dinner. I said yes because I wanted to find out more about what happened at the foot fetish parties; why young women and normal looking professional white-collar men attended. He said many college-aged girls were doing this to pay their tuition—not the foot modeling, but full-on sex.

Marcus asked me many times to have sex for $100.00/hour. For a 19-year-old, whose only experience so far was working in exchange for $3.00/hour, $100.00/hour in my mind was the equivalent to being rich.

I turned his offer down.

On that day, I vowed I would never earn money in a way that would violate or compromise my values. I refused to be like those college girls selling their body to pay tuition. I would have rather worked at Starbucks.

We live in a culture where news articles glorify the former nurse Allie Rae who quit her full-time job because she makes

$75,000.00 a month from Only Fans. Many people call this a form of "female empowerment."

This is bullshit!

Anyone who disagrees with this mainstream trend, including me, gets labeled conservative.

It's disgusting for a woman to do that.

Women have more value than that.

Our predecessors fought so hard for women to have the right to vote, earn money, and open our own bank accounts.

How on earth do women today believe the only way for them to have a lot of money is to either prostitute themselves, inherit a fortune, or marry rich?

The saddest thing is looks have an expiration date.

After turning 30, how will these women earn money and support themselves?

What about STDs and STIs?

And what man would want to marry and have kids with a woman who doesn't respect herself?

After dinner with Marcus, I made a vow:

I refuse to make money from my body!

I am not a piece of meat!

I have a brain and that's how I'm going to make money.

I'm going to make money and create the life of my dreams solely with the power of my mind.

And men and women in our society will come to know me for my intellect and creativity.

Going forward, I would never turn my back against my morals and my beliefs in the slightest, even if that meant losing my job or letting a big opportunity slip through my fingers.

I would rather work for $8.00/hour doing the most repetitive, mundane, boring work than ever commit an act that would eat away at my soul for the rest of my life. So that's exactly what I did—I worked a whole string of minimum wage jobs until I discovered my calling. And after I discovered my calling, I committed 100%.

I'm telling you. I really love money, but you couldn't pay me a million dollars to do something that feels wrong to my core. That's why I never take sponsors on my YouTube channel. I have only ever accepted one sponsorship, and that was for a bank that lets you open a checking account without a social security number—which is a great financial product for immigrants—but they went out of business last year. No one could ever pay me enough to say things about a financial product I don't truly believe in. This is why people have so much trust in me. I never compromise.

I share this story because there's something I realized through the years: once you accept money for doing a job you can't get behind 100%, there is no going back. You can't return the money and get your conscience back.

The lesson is even in the Bible. Judas betrayed Jesus by handing him over to the chief priests for only 30 pieces of silver. Filled with remorse, he tried to return the 30 silver coins, but he could do nothing at that point. What's done is done. He dumped the coins in the temple and then hung himself.

Chapter 11

Aligning Actions and Words for Personal Integrity

When I made the vow to quit any job that asked me to do things I personally found wrong, I placed a lot of faith in God to take care of me and protect me. God is my financial provider, not man. God simply works through man as a vehicle to give me money.

I actually followed through with my vow. I was working full-time at a hardware store. My friend from China needed a job, so I asked the store manager if he could hook her up for a job with one of our vendors. He called up his contacts and one of them was hiring. He drove my friend to the interview. When he returned, he talked about how pretty she was and how he wanted to have sex with her. He even pulled out a condom from his pocket.

This was a moment when my personal values were put to the test. Knowing what you stand for in such situations, and being firm in your convictions, that's what makes all the difference. That's what guided me then, and if you're unsure about your personal values, I've created something to help. The Standing Firm: Defining Your Personal Core Values Exercise, available on my website annieyangfinancial.com/core-values, might just give you the clarity you need.

Normally, I don't care about this stuff. But he asked me specifically to not tell her he's been married for 20 years and is the father of eight kids. I said I wouldn't go out of my way to tell her, but that if she asked, I would only speak the truth. I don't lie to my friends.

Lo and behold, she asked me about him, so I told her the truth. I told her to keep quiet about what I said because I didn't want to be blamed, but after she canceled the date, the store manager was angry. She never said it was because of me, but he assumed it was because of me. And he assumed right.

On Saturday, when I wasn't at work, the store manager called me and cursed me for half an hour. He gaslighted me. He said he never intended to have sex with her and that he just wanted to be friends. He denied pulling a condom out of his pocket three days before. He called me all kinds of horrible names. He even attacked my integrity. He said that I think I'm so righteous and that I have so much integrity and character, but I'm a horrible person on the inside because I ruined his happiness! I said, "I'm sorry, but I don't do things that are against my values." Still, he wouldn't forgive me and just kept cursing repeatedly.

I contemplated quitting my job. On Monday, I told my boss (the company owner) about what the store manager did to me over the weekend. My boss didn't want to take sides, and he didn't know how to handle the situation since it wasn't a work-related issue, so he just said not to take it too personally.

I thought about it some more and decided I didn't want to work with someone who asked me to lower my personal standards. The next day I gave a two weeks' notice to resign. Every day, for two weeks, my boss begged me to stay. He offered me better pay… better hours… to let me work upstairs instead of inside the store with the store manager.

It was not good enough for me!

Even though I didn't have another job lined up, I didn't care!

I had a six-month emergency fund.

So, I said good riddance!

Chapter 12

Trusting in Divine Providence
for Your Career Success

The same day I gave my two weeks' notice, my property manager, Anthony, called me. He asked how I was doing and what I was up to. I thought, *this is the worst timing.* If I openly told my property manager that I had just quit my job with nothing lined up, he was going to think that I was financially irresponsible and unable to pay my rent.

Turned out the phone call was a miracle. He said he was calling me because he wanted to offer me a job. Anthony wanted me to assist him in property management part-time and in exchange for the work, I could live rent free. My rent was $750.00. I spent only around $425.00/month on everything outside of rent, and my transportation cost was $0.00 since I biked everywhere for free. This arrangement meant that I could live on my emergency funds at a rate of only $425.00/month. It was a sign from God that I had done the right thing.

I was set to start classes at Kingsborough Community College the next month. Instead of immediately looking for another job, I used that time to relax and reflect. I could figure out how to find a new job later. But after I began school, another miracle happened. The tuition was really cheap. My full Pell Grant and NY Tap Grant paid the whole tuition because of my low income status, and they directly deposited the remaining funds into my bank account for me to spend on anything. I got around $3,500.00 per semester in cash. I withdrew \$800.00/month to cover my necessities and hobbies and never dipped into my emergency fund at all.

I was still stingy with my budgeting. I budgeted \$30.00/week for groceries and there was one week when I hadn't planned well enough. I didn't have enough food to eat on only \$30.00 that week. I was starving after finishing a class.

A classmate I had never spoken to before approached me and said he wanted to get to know me more. In conversation, I told him I really liked to save money and he asked if I could help him make a budget. We sat down, and I made a budget for him. I asked him how much he paid for his phone bill. I forgot the amount, but I showed him how he could cut his phone bill by 50%.

It was such a revelation for him that the budget was reasonable and doable, and that he could actually save money while living comfortably. He said he was so grateful, he wanted to buy me a meal. I never told him I was starving, but I ended up getting exactly what I needed at just the right time.

This is just one story out of many in my life. It's almost like, no matter what happens to me, my needs are always met in the strangest coincidences without money needing to change hands. Or is it a coincidence? Don't be afraid to follow your calling and speak your truth. When you're on the right path, everything will go your way. You will always be provided for.

Life should feel effortless.

It's when you're on the wrong path that it feels like you're swimming against the current.

Part 2

Preparation

"I will study and prepare myself, and someday my chance will come."

—Abraham Lincoln

Chapter 13

Personal Branding: Standing Out in the Job Market

Personal branding makes up 50% of your success in landing a job quickly. It's the reason incompetent people get hired at work. They know how to sell themselves.

Branding and marketing are not sleazy and selfish. If you really believe in your work, and you have a calling, you must tell everyone in the world what it is so that you can further that purpose. If no one knows what you're here to do, no one will consider you for opportunities.

When you're looking for your future spouse on a dating app, you're vetting people before you even go on the first date. You search the name on Google and look them up on social media just to do your due diligence. You want to make sure this isn't some psychopath or sex offender or narcissist or any other form of crazy.

Employers do the same. They check you out before they message you. No one wants to hire a crazy freak who will end up going on a mass shooting rampage to exact revenge over some petty problem at work.

Aside from that, think of the first date. First dates are awkward. What if you find out you both have nothing in common and you can't find anything to talk about? What are you going to do? Are you going to get up after 30 minutes and say, "Hey, sorry.

We're not the right fit. I'm going to go now." Chances are, you were raised to be more polite than that, so you'll ride it out.

Job interviews can feel just as awkward as first dates. Thirty minutes into the interview, the interviewer isn't going to say you're not what they're looking for and show you the door. It's rude. They have to ride it out and say, "We'll contact you and let you know in a few days," even when it's a clear no. To avoid this awkwardness, they want to do all their due diligence before giving you an interview. If you have your personal brand online, you're making their due diligence process easier.

Companies also don't have all the time in the world to do interviews. If there are ten suitable candidates in a pool of 300 applicants, and they interviewed all ten, it'd be a ten-hour process. They need to cut the list down to five and you want to be in that short list.

I guarantee you will land a job in five days if you follow my instructions on personal branding to the letter and build a stellar reputation over the next five years. Think of all the people who are incredibly famous and well respected in their industry. Do you think they ever have problems landing a job offer? Do you think they need to wait three months before hearing back from a company? No. They get a phone call right away. Every company wants to snatch this person up before someone else. If it's possible for famous people, why isn't it possible for you?

Chapter 14

Balancing Authenticity and Professionalism at Work

Bring your entire self to work. I don't mean to wear your heart on your sleeve and tell everyone about your private matters. You can maintain your professionalism while also bringing your personality, values, and beliefs to work, and people will love you for it. People are not robots, yet our society teaches people they need to be generic and politically friendly at work. When you do this, you become bland. You never stand out. People who become successful embrace their uniqueness and aren't afraid to share it with enthusiasm.

It wasn't until I met my dentist, Dr. Valdemar Welz, that I realized you can be professional while also being personal. He passed away last year, but he has left a lasting impression on me. He was more than a dentist to me. He was an inspiration. I will remember him for the rest of my life.

How did I end up meeting Dr. Welz?

Prior to becoming his patient, I had two adjacent fillings done by a dentist who graduated from Columbia University College of Dental Medicine. He completed the shoddy work on my teeth in the record time of half an hour. The fillings fell out two weeks later when I flossed. An Ivy League education is not a guaranteed sign of a great dentist.

I had to get my fillings redone by a different dentist who was busy talking to her assistant about her vacation in Spain while working on my teeth for one hour. After that, I had on and off pain in that area of my mouth for an entire year. I went back to her twice complaining about the pain, but she said it was just my sinuses and that I probably had a cold and the pain would go away. The pain never went away.

I complained about my pain to a colleague of mine. She told me that her father was a former dentist and did all her fillings when she was a kid. Her father filled her teeth with gold. And apparently, the work was so beautiful that whenever she got her teeth cleaned by a new dentist, the dentist would ask everyone in the office to gather around and take pictures of the fillings.

I had never heard of gold fillings before. None of my past dentists ever offered them. Apparently, it's a well-known secret among dentists that gold is the highest standard you could opt for. Gold is the best material because it's non-reactive (therefore, no pain) and isn't sensitive to changes in temperature when you eat and drink hot or cold foods. Done well, gold fillings can last your entire lifetime. Your family members can even take it out after you die and sell it for money.

I called 30 dentists in Boston asking if they did gold fillings and they all said no. Finally, I came across Dr. Welz. To my knowledge, he was the only dentist in town that did gold fillings (since I stopped calling more dentists after that). Dr. Welz was well known for his expertise and had been doing gold fillings for over 30 years. Satisfied with his background, I booked an appointment.

When I first walked into Dr. Welz's office, it didn't feel like a dentist's office. In the spacious waiting room were shelves upon shelves of his favorite health, theology, and personal development books. He designed the waiting room like an art gallery with gold framed paintings hanging on the walls. The table lamps emitted a warm hue, a stark difference from the cool white ceiling lights you would typically find in office buildings and hospitals. The sofas were so soft, I wanted to sleep there. There was a fireplace for me to warm my hands. Classical music played in the background. It was almost like I was being invited into someone's home.

To become Dr. Welz's patient, I had to do a mandatory two-hour orientation session. He explained the anatomy of teeth, the causes of tooth decay, how I should brush my teeth with a timer for four minutes twice a day, which toothpaste to use, and more. Beyond teeth, he shared his love for veganism and nutrition. At 69 years old, he was full of energy and vitality. The welcome packet included a beautiful poem penned by his daughter, a book about why patients keep getting cavities and what to do about it, and a goody bag with a toothbrush and floss. Prior to Dr. Welz, I never had a dentist take this much time to educate me on how to take care of my teeth.

Dr. Welz took an x-ray and showed me the mistake the second dentist made that was causing the pain. I had to redo the fillings to get rid of the pain. I opted for gold this time.

It was a two-visit procedure. During the first visit, Dr. Welz spent three hours working on my teeth. He diligently removed all the decay and cleaned the teeth before putting in the temporary fillings. He took several molds to make sure the filling would be accurate. During the second visit, he again spent three hours working on my teeth. He kept putting the gold fillings in, testing them, and taking them back out several times, shaving them down to the perfect fit before permanently gluing them in place.

I asked him why he took so long to work on my teeth. He told me he was already working the fastest he could. He couldn't work any faster than that. But then I told him that the last two dentists did my fillings in under an hour, so was he lying? He said that they learned the same things he did in dental school. The difference was that they chose not to follow the right procedures. If those dentists actually followed every single procedure they were supposed to follow as they learned in school, they would take just as long to do the work. They were cutting corners here and there and not giving patients highly focused attention, which resulted in poorly done fillings that fell out after only five years.

I asked him why he wasn't cutting corners like everyone else. To which he responded, "God gave me the gift of dexterity. He already gave you perfect teeth, but you didn't take care of your teeth and you ate processed foods, so they decayed. I am using my God given gift to restore your teeth to be almost as good as your original, but the restorations will never be as perfect as the original. Regardless, I will give it my best effort and do it to the best of my abilities." I finally understood. For him, his life's work was a calling. And while he served dental patients, he spread the message of God. He loved God and he shared his love with all his patients while they laid in the dental chair. At Dr. Welz's funeral, there were over 100 attendees. Loved ones shared stories about how he was not only committed to delivering outstanding work, but he was also a devout lover of God and veganism and never felt afraid to share it. If you had just met him, you would hear about God less than five minutes into the conversation. He touched the lives of many people.

I was so inspired by how Dr. Welz lived his life that I wanted to follow in his footsteps. Two weeks after he passed away, I fell asleep and dreamed that I got a phone call from a private number. I answered the call and on the other end was Dr. Welz's voice. He said he got my email about looking for a new dentist and needing a recommendation. It was true. I had just emailed his office two days earlier. He gave me a name in Boston, but I didn't need the information anymore because I decided to look for a dentist in New York City. I was insistent on finding a replacement dentist that also did gold fillings. I asked him how he was feeling because he had just passed away two weeks prior. He said he was transitioning fine, but he was just wrapping up a few things to make sure everything was running smoothly without him. He ended with, "If you ever need anything, Annie, you can always call me and I'll answer."

I woke up from the dream and emailed the office explaining what happened. His daughter responded to my email saying it really was Dr. Welz speaking to me. He *always* said that last line to his patients. I didn't know he had a habit of saying that while he was alive because I had only done five visits with him before he passed away.

A few months later, my piano teacher put together a student recital. I had never performed piano in front of other people before and I was feeling nervous and anxious about it. I felt scared I would make a mistake and make a fool out of myself in front of everyone.

Two days before the recital while I was eating lunch, Dr. Welz's spirit spoke to me again. It was distinctly his voice inside my head—no mistaking it. He said, "Annie, just like how I shared my love for God and veganism when I was alive, you must share your love for the piano with the world. It doesn't matter whether you make a mistake. It's not even about playing the pieces perfectly. The most important thing is that you share your love, your passion, your joy for the music and for the piano." While hearing his message, inside my heart I felt the same warmth and protection I felt while lying in his dental chair.

After I got his message, I calmed down a lot. You need to hear this message as well. Don't be afraid to share yourself. You can be an outstanding service professional and share your passions with the people around you, just like Dr. Welz.

Chapter 15

Curating Your Online Narrative With Your Full Name

Annie Margarita Yang. My entire life, I went by Annie Yang. I wanted to develop an online presence, so I decided the best way to achieve that was by using Annie Margarita Yang across all my profiles online. It was a strategic decision in my journey to personally brand myself.

It was a smart decision because there are plenty of Annie Yangs. If you google, "Annie Yang," a bunch of different search results show up. If you google, "Annie Margarita Yang," I dominate all the regular search results, including the image search results. If you have a middle name, you are lucky. I recommend you include your middle name in all your online profiles.

I wanted to control the narrative for my life story online and the only way to do that was to dominate the search results with my own curated content. When I googled myself early on, I came across things I wrote back when I was 13 years old on Yahoo! Answers. My answers to questions like, "Why do we like to stay under warm fuzzy blankets instead of getting out of bed?" Cringy.

I fixed it by googling my old username handles and my name, to find old accounts on websites. I used the "forgot password" reset link on all the sites to log in and closed all the accounts. After a few months, they were removed from the Google search results.

An example of someone who doesn't control his online narrative is my boss. I googled his name for the fun of it. He's not active on any social media—the profile photo is blank for any social media he has. What popped up was a photo of him at City Hall with a mask on because it was COVID-19. Another photo was of him from 10 years ago at a baseball game. And lastly, there was a news article about how he planned to demolish a building and replace it with a new building. There was a blog with commenters slandering his good name by calling him a bunch of horrible things for wanting to "gentrify and ruin the neighborhood." Another person in the comments defended him, saying he was a really nice guy. If you don't control your online narrative, other people will. You don't get to opt out of this.

You need to make sure your real name, your username handles, and your URLs all match across the internet. This way, people will become familiar with you. They'll begin associating your name, your username, and your URLs with your work.

Chapter 16

Creating a Lasting First Impression With a Professional Headshot

Your photo is the first impression that you make. The picture communicates to everyone what kind of person you are. You want your photo to look absolutely amazing because you, my friend, are most likely amazing to work with. You just need your photo to show it.

Hire a professional photographer who specializes in headshots. Don't use your cousin or your acquaintance who does photography as a hobby so that you can save money. Don't use a photographer whose primary source of income is wedding photographs. When I say headshots, I mean headshots. This is your future career. If you use someone who doesn't specialize in headshots, then you are not taking your career seriously.

Please don't skimp on this. If it's too expensive for you, then save up money over the course of a few months. It's better to wait a few months to have a high-quality headshot that highlights your gorgeous smile and personality than a headshot that simply looks okay. When I researched headshot photographers in Boston, I narrowed my choices down to three. The one I ended up going with was the most expensive one. If you're wondering who, it was Ryuji Suzuki from Beaupix Studio for Headshots & Portraits in Boston (beaupix.com). He charged $300.00 versus the others who charged only $150.00 to $200.00. I had to budget and save for this because I was working at an entry-level accounting job at the time. The reason I went with the most expensive one was because he promised to do more than simply take a flattering picture of me. He promised that my personality and my character would shine through in the photo. He also promised to take a photo for the job I wanted, not for the job I had. I told him to make me look like a future CFO. It was like taking a bet on myself, hoping it would all be worth it, and it paid off. Looking back, this was one of the best things I spent my money on for my career.

How do you know you've found a great headshot photographer? Headshot photography is a tough business to succeed in. How many headshots does the average person need? Only one. This means there is very little repeat business, so it's hard to make a living unless the photographer is frugal enough with money to survive the initial years. If the photographer has a comprehensive headshot portfolio on his website and is still in business after 10 years, he's superb.

According to Ryuji, 80% of taking a beautiful headshot comes from the preparation work before arriving at the studio. The photographer's magic is the remaining 20%. You don't just show up at the studio and out comes this gorgeous picture of you. No amount of Photoshop can fix you if you didn't look gorgeous to begin with. It's not about being born with the right genes. You just need to look healthy and take care of yourself.

Here's the advice Ryuji gave me.

In the Weeks Leading Up to the Photoshoot:

- *Shop For Your Outfit:* Try on many outfits. There are some colors that make your skin look dull and sick. Wear a color that flatters and brightens up your skin.

Three Days Leading Up to the Photoshoot:

- *Drink Water*: Drink lots of water so your skin will be hydrated.
- *Moisturize*: You need moisturized skin in order for your makeup to avoid looking cakey.
- *Apply Chapstick*: Lipstick can't cover up chapped, flakey lips.
- *Sleep*: Sleep at the same time every day and get your full eight hours of sleep. You don't want eyebags and dark under-eye circles in your photo.
- *Relax*: Take a hot bath to relax your muscles. Do yoga to stretch everything out. Do self-massage all over your body and especially self-massage your face every few hours, so your forehead and jaw muscles will be relaxed in the photo. You can't hide stress and tension with Photoshop.

On the Night Before Your Photoshoot:

- *Iron Your Outfit*: Remove all the wrinkles from your clothes so it looks nice and crisp. Make sure your outfit doesn't have any stains.

On the Day of Your Photoshoot:

- *Cut Your Hair*: Make sure you schedule your appointment for early in the morning right before the photoshoot. If you don't get a fresh haircut, your hair will look limp. If a haircut is too much for you, you can trim and style your hair at the salon. You want to look like you're someone who takes great care of yourself because if you don't, you will send the wrong message.
- *Do Your Makeup*: This applies to both men and women. Studio lights are very bright and you'll look washed out like a ghost if you don't wear makeup. You can either use the professional makeup artist that partners with the photographer, hire your own makeup artist, or do your own

makeup if you're confident in your skills. If you plan on doing it yourself, practice doing makeup for the camera. Camera makeup and real-life makeup are completely different. That's why you see those beauty influencers packing on the makeup in their videos, but if you followed what they did, it'd look cakey in real life. They're not doing it on purpose—it's because it won't show up properly on the camera unless they cake that stuff on.

During the Photoshoot:

Your only job is to be natural. Be authentic. Be yourself. Your photographer is going to ask you a bunch of questions about your life while taking pictures of you. Remember to smile with your teeth while talking. People who smile with their teeth look more friendly and welcoming to talk to than those who don't. The kinds of questions Ryuji asked me were about my interests, my passions, my goals, and my visions for my future. He looked for topics that made me super excited, so my eyes naturally lit up. That's how he captured the passion, enthusiasm, and charisma in my eyes. You want employers to look at your photo and believe you're the right one for the job because passion can take people very far. The owner of the company told our mutual friend (I didn't even know we had one) that I had a lot of passion for my work when he interviewed me. "Her passion won me over."

After the Photoshoot:

Change every single one of your profile pictures on the internet to your new professional headshot. Yes, even your personal social media. Like it or not, employers look at your personal social media before reaching out for an interview. You want to be instantly recognizable everywhere on the Internet. You want people to look at your photo and immediately recognize who you are simply by the photo, without reading your name.

I was looking to hire an architect for structural drawings for my balcony. A contractor referred me to an architect through a text message so I didn't get her last name. She told me she wanted a payment deposit via Venmo. Her last name on Venmo was "Architect." When she emailed me, the last name in her email was "Architect." Her email signature was blank.

It was very difficult for me to figure out exactly who she was and whether she was qualified for this project. The only photo I had was her Venmo profile picture. I googled her first name and the word "Architect" and "Boston" to see if anything would come up. I found a LinkedIn profile and it looked like her, but I wasn't sure. The Venmo picture looked like it was taken in a different year from the LinkedIn picture. I know that the shape of people's eyebrows almost never changes, and the eyebrow shape was the same, so I was 80% sure that it was her. But I can't say 100%.

You want to avoid being in the same position as this architect. Change every single picture to be your one headshot. People won't remember your name, but they'll remember your photo. This is your way of saying hello to the world. And if you do amazing work, the world won't stop talking about you.

Do this even for sites and software that are not related to job opportunities. You never know who might introduce you to your next opportunity. So going forward, put the same picture on any website that lets you upload a profile picture.

Chapter 17

Telling Your Unique Story Through Personal Branding

For your personal brand, you first have to decide on a color palette and second on a typeface. I suggest you hire a graphic designer to choose your personal brand. I don't have an eye for art and design so I could never get this right.

Color communicates a message. The color palette isn't a matter of choosing your favorite colors and making them look good together. There is a reason big corporations, like McDonalds, spent a lot of time choosing the color for their brand. Color communicates a message.

What are you trying to communicate about yourself? Before you can answer this question clearly, you need to know yourself well, and I've got a tool that might just help. Head on over to annieyangfinancial.com/personal-branding and download the Carving Your Mark: A Personal Branding Worksheet. It's an opportunity for you to dive deep into what makes you, you.

Explain to your graphic designer what you're trying to communicate about yourself. For example, when I first started working with my graphic designer, Luis Guadalupe, I told him that this was what I wanted the world to know about me:

I'm the girl next door. I am the child of working-class Chinese immigrants. I worked minimum wage job after minimum wage job. I speak to Millennials in a similar position. I'm pretty much average. The only difference between me and other people is I have big dreams and an out-

standing work ethic. If I can do it, anyone else can. I'm frugal. I only spend money according to my priorities, goals, and values. I care about delivering high-quality work. I like to spend money on services and products that are of high quality. When people see me online, I want them to think I'm inspiring, funny, informative, authentic, simple, inviting, and practical. I am not superior to anyone.

Luis chose a beautiful teal and gold for my personal brand. After I formed Annie Yang Financial Corporation, I told him to change the colors to match the new vibe: an extremely professional and well-trusted company. Every client we service is in excellent hands. He changed the brand to navy and gold.

For the typeface, Steve Jobs's story best illustrates the importance. One of the most transformative life experiences for Steve Jobs was during the few months after he dropped out of Reed College. Since he no longer needed to take specific classes to graduate, he dropped into whichever classes piqued his interest and curiosity (with the professors' permission). One of them was a calligraphy class, and in his 2005 Stanford commencement speech, he shared,

"I learned about serif and sans serif typefaces, about how to vary the amount of space between different letter combinations, about what makes great typeface great. It was beautiful, historical, artistically subtle in a way that science can't capture, and I found it fascinating."

He drew upon his fascination ten years later when he designed the first Macintosh with beautiful typography.

Typography communicates. Have you ever seen a book cover with text only—no illustrations? It's a minimalist design, yet the designer got the reader's attention to consider buying the book.

I'm not an expert on typeface—I only know it's important. I stressed the importance to Luis about getting this right for my personal brand. Do the same when you're discussing this project with your graphic designer.

After Luis created my personal brand, I started using it for everything. Think of anything that you can design that incorporates your personal brand. Over the years, the things that came to mind were my website, business cards, email signature, letterhead, social media, thank you cards, happy birthday cards, and even gift wrap paper and bow and ribbon. You want people to recognize you on the Internet with your photo, and you want people to recognize you from the personal brand alone. So even if your name and photo are missing, they can still identify you.

Chapetr 18

Optimizing Your LinkedIn Profile to Maximize Interview Requests

Thoroughly complete your entire LinkedIn profile to get All-Star status. A thoroughly completed profile communicates that you care. If you're that thorough in completing your profile, people assume you're just as thorough in your work.

When I was creating my LinkedIn profile, I thought I needed to work in my field for several years before I could attain All-Star status. I realized it was a false belief. The profile was just marketing, so you can attain All-Star status even as a fresh college graduate working an entry-level job.

If you're having a tough time wrapping your head around all this, or you simply want to ensure that you're leveraging LinkedIn's potential to the fullest, I've got something to help. Pop over to annieyangfinancial.com/linkedin-checklist and download the Maximizing Your Professional Image: A LinkedIn Profile Optimization Checklist. I designed this checklist as a road map, guiding you step by step towards a polished and powerful LinkedIn presence that can open doors for you.

If you think the time isn't now and that it's somewhere in the far-off future when you're more "qualified" to have an All-Star status, I have a question for you. At what point will you be qualified? I kept waiting and waiting, thinking it would be someday.

That someday came when I achieved the internal barometer that I created for myself a few years earlier. My mind moved the bar again, resulting in my new someday being pushed further back into the future. Now is the best time to do it even if you think you lack enough content to put on your profile. You have more than enough content if you give this your best shot. Hustle.

This is how opportunity happens: You complete your profile 100%. Someone is hunting for the best person for a brand-new opportunity. The job listing isn't posted yet because he doesn't want to sift through 300+ applications. This manager is just curious and is privately looking around to see if there are highly qualified people who can help him make the new project a success. This person reaches out to you specifically. Why? Because he learned about your skills and experience before even having a conversation. This has happened to me many times. All because I attained All-Star status. There are plenty of people much smarter than me, but I get contacted all the time about a lot of new opportunities because people see what I'm capable of through a quick search.

How do you get All-Star status? It's easy. I recommend you get the free 30-day trial of LinkedIn Premium. This will allow you to view profiles of other professionals in your industry without being connected. You check out what they are doing for inspiration. Note precisely what made the great-looking profiles so great, and what made the mediocre profiles mediocre. Here's what I found based on my observations:

Profile Picture

Upload the professional headshot. Make sure you crop the photo so that the bottom edge ends right below your shoulders. The picture is small, so you want to make sure everyone can see your beautiful face!

Headline

The mediocre profiles simply used their title and company. You don't have to use the default. You have a 120-character limit. You can use the headline to communicate what you do and who you help, such as, "Helping first-time homebuyers find their dream home," or "Writing professional bios for IT professionals," or "Financial planning for Millennials to retire early." These are way more attractive headlines than the boring title & company that everyone else uses.

Experience

This section describes all the job positions you've worked along with supporting information. Since your LinkedIn profile is not a resume, it doesn't make sense to do bullet points. You are crafting the story of your past career. Use this section to write a paragraph. Answer these questions:

- What product or service did the company sell to make money? It's not always obvious to outsiders, so make it clear on your profile.
- What was it like before you worked there?
- What projects did you work on?
- How did you make a difference?
- What did you accomplish?

It's important to frame your experience in a way that communicates how you always left a company better than you found it. Employers are going to read and think that if you took ownership and responsibility in previous positions, then you'll act that way when you work for them, too.

Skills

You can add up to 50 skills. Many people don't know this, but recruiters search based on skills to find potential candidates. If you don't put anything here, you're decreasing your chances of showing up in search results. How do you determine what skills to put? Easy. With your 30-day free trial of LinkedIn Premium, you can search for other professionals just like recruiters do!

Search for profiles with the job title you are aiming to land, and open 100 profiles in a new tab. Scroll to the skills section of each profile and copy and paste their skills into an Excel sheet. After you're done, sort the list from A-Z and remove duplicates. Now you have an entire list of skills to draw from. Highlight the skills you actually have—don't overthink it. And then, looking at your new filtered list, look for the skills that are highly technical and in demand in your industry. Those definitely need to be on your profile. If your list of skills doesn't add up to 50 yet, look at the list again for the soft skills you have. The soft skills should be relevant to the job title you're looking to land.

Summary

I always struggled with this part. I couldn't create a professional bio that was concise, showcased why I was so amazing, and explained what kind of new opportunities I was open to. If I struggled with this, I'm sure you would struggle with this as well.

I hired a copywriter named Cheril Clarke from Phenomenal Writing LLC (phenomenalwriting.com). She asked me questions about my background and which direction I wanted to take my career, looked at my existing LinkedIn profile, my website, and social media, and wrote an amazing bio for me. She wrote a long version and a short version, and I used the short version whenever I had character limits. She's more expensive than other copywriters, but she's written bios for CEOs and executives, so that's why I recommend her.

When I was doing my research and shopping around, many copywriters were actually faceless companies where you didn't know who was writing your bio. It could have been an intern or maybe outsourced. I'm not saying they can't do quality copywriting, but I was concerned because I didn't want someone to take my career and put it into a cookie cutter template. I wanted my bio to stand out from the crowd. Just like the professional head-shot, invest more money in this to get a better-quality result.

Put your email address at the end of your summary. In the contact section of LinkedIn, only connections can see your email address. If you put it in the summary section, everyone can see it regardless of whether you're connected.

Industry & Location

This one is easy. You can figure this out.

Education

This one is easy as well. You could put the graduation year if you graduated recently and your profile is sparse. It would help explain why your profile isn't extensive.

Connections

You need at least 50 connections to attain All-Star status. Connect with everyone you know, even acquaintances. I amassed thousands of connections by taking advantage of the LinkedIn Premium trial and reaching out to other professionals in the industry with a message that I wanted to grow my network without sounding too salesy. And if you're wondering how to approach this without sounding too pushy, well, I've got a resource that could be of immense help. Swing by annieyangfinancial.com/linkedin-messages and download the Personalized LinkedIn Connection Message Templates. Crafted with utmost care, these templates are your secret weapon to make an impactful, genuine connection. You'd be surprised at how many people respond positively! Give it a shot.

URL

Customize your LinkedIn URL to something short and easy, like your name. You'll be putting this link in your resume header later.

Banner

Ask your graphic designer to design your LinkedIn banner using your personal brand. Most people use the default blue banner. To really stand out, you need to do this. Make sure you test the banner on both your desktop and the LinkedIn mobile app. The profile picture overlaps a part of the banner in both versions, and you want to make sure the profile picture doesn't block anything important, like text.

Chapter 19

Securing Your Digital Real Estate With a Personal Domain Name

If you're lucky enough that your (FirstName)(LastName).com is still available, buy it immediately.

If not, try these variations:

- (FirstName)(MiddleInitial)(LastName).com
- (FirstInitial)(LastName).com
- (FirstInitial)(MiddleInitial)(LastName).com
- (FirstName)(MiddleName)(LastName).com

If all else fails, you can always copy the celebrities:

- The(FirstName)(LastName).com
- (FirstName)(LastName)Official.com

An owner has been squatting AnnieYang.com since 2005. There is no website on AnnieYang.com. I paid a domain broker $99.00 to negotiate a sale. After back-and-forth negotiation, the owner said he would sell it for $5,000.00. No thanks.

I bought AnnieMargaritaYang.com on Google Domains for $12.00. I could have gone with AMYang.com, but I didn't want people to think my name was Am. AnnieMargaritaYang.com is long but that's never stopped me from building an online presence. Outside of big websites like Facebook, Instagram, etc., no one types the website URL nowadays. They type what they think they're looking for into Google and then click the link. The older generation believes Google *is* the Internet.

Chapter 20

Designing an Affordable and Effective Personal Website

You can easily create a website with drag-and-drop builders, such as Squarespace ($16.00/month) and Wix ($16.00/month). These website builders already have beautiful templates you can use for the basic structure. You can change the typography and colors to match your personal brand. You can have a website up by the end of the day.

Your website doesn't need to be complicated. An "About" page that includes your photo and professional bio, a "Portfolio" page (if you're creative), and a "Contact" page is enough, along with links to your LinkedIn and professional social media in either the header or footer.

Chapter 21

Registering a Custom Domain Email Address for Free

The great thing about a custom domain name email address is that people will infer you have a website, even if you don't tell them. Get an email address with your custom domain name. It's more professional than a Gmail / Microsoft / Yahoo / AOL / Comcast email address. People will type your domain name into the address bar and check out your website out of curiosity.

You have two options.

You can either pay $6.00/month for Google Workspace to go with your custom domain name. With Google Workspace, you get more than just an email—you get an entire suite of Google's productivity tools.

Or you can do the free option, which is you use your personal Gmail and set up your custom domain name email address as an alias. The best way I can describe it is you keep using your personal Gmail, but you can "send email as" and "reply to email as" your custom domain name email address. You can watch YouTube videos on how to do this. They explain it better.

Chapter 22

Expanding Your Network With a Professional Email Signature

A professional email signature is another way to display what you do. Even if you're not emailing someone who is in charge of hiring for an open position, you never really know who you're emailing and who might provide you with your next job opportunity. That person may know someone who knows someone, who knows someone hiring. The more people know about you, the more likely they are to recommend you to others. People absolutely love it when they make a great referral for someone and then get praise and credit for making the introduction.

Whenever you send an email with your custom domain name email address, even if it's not work-related, people will look at your email signature. And if there are links in your email signature, they will click on them. This was my thought all these years, but it actually wasn't until last month when I got cold hard proof that my thinking was correct.

I emailed my insurance agent because I wanted to buy personal umbrella insurance. After I got my new policy, she emailed me to thank me for choosing their company and that she saw in my email signature that I am an author. She checked out my book, *1001 Ways to Save Money* (on Amazon), and told the company book club members that her client was an author. They all bought copies of my book and are reading it for their next book club meeting.

Now that you're convinced to get yours done, I recommend you check out www.signature.email for your professional email signature. I love saving money, so I already did all the research on the cheapest option. This company lets you design one email signature for only a one-time fee of $19.00. All the other companies charge a subscription.

Remember to include your professional headshot, personal brand colors, your website URL, LinkedIn profile URL, and other social media URLs in your email signature. Ask your graphic designer to design this if you need help.

Chapter 23

Demonstrating Your Expertise Through Valuable Content

Create something on the Internet that people can check out. You can write a few articles and make a few videos every so often in your area of expertise to showcase your knowledge. The purpose isn't to build a following and become a full-time professional content creator—it's to build the perception that you have authority and expertise on this subject so that you can land a job.

You also don't have to stick to only creating content related to your work. It could be anything. If you recently gained an interest in gardening, you could do something with that. For me, it's piano. As I'm writing this, I'm in the process of creating ThePiano-Journal.com so that I can publicly document my journey to 10,000 piano practice hours. I enjoy learning new things and teaching what I learned as I go. I have found that when you teach a subject, you gain the most. If you learn something by yourself, you hear it only once. But when you teach it again and again, you hear it every time while everyone else listening has heard it only once. In the end, you gain a deep understanding of the subject.

It's easy to write a couple of articles. If you finished college, you had to write essays all the time. You clearly have the skill to do it.

The problem is mindset. Maybe you're self-conscious. Maybe you think your work isn't good enough. Don't hold back. Everyone was a beginner at some point. Sometimes, it's actually a good thing you're not a total expert at something because with an intermediate understanding of a subject, you're better suited to teach a beginner. You know how to dumb down the material.

Some experts are so advanced in their knowledge, it's hard for me to understand what they are teaching because they assume I have already learned the foundational basics. So long as you know a little more than the next guy, you're qualified to teach. When you help enough people, one day when you need something, people will go out of their way to help you in return.

Neil Patel, an authority on Internet marketing, talked about this on a podcast. He was studying for an architecture exam and he documented what resources he used when he was studying. He wrote blog posts about what he learned. And a few months later, he passed the exam and forgot all about the website. After getting laid off, he learned a bit more about Internet marketing. He connected an analytical tool to his website and discovered that thousands of people were visiting his website every single day and were sharing the link to his site in online forums. He took the content and organized it into an eBook to help people study more efficiently. In the first month, he made $8,000.00 in sales. Many people emailed him saying they bought the eBook even though they already passed the exam because they wanted to pay him for his free help. Prior to creating the eBook, he had no way of getting paid. Neil's story is an example of equal exchange.

Similarly, there is a podcast called The Life Coach School Podcast by Brooke Castillo. Her free work is so valuable—it's changed my life. If her stuff is free, why would I pay for it? My philosophy is that if her free work is this good, can you imagine how much better her paid work must be? I ended up spending $1,188.00 on her courses. It's true! Her paid content is like the free content on steroids. Whenever you give information away for free, it will always come back to you tenfold.

I was giving examples of businesspeople selling courses online, but the same concept applies to people looking to land a job. It's a fundamental core truth. Building authority, so that people literally want to throw their wallet at you.

Blogging

No one reads blogs anymore. Big corporations have gamed the Google search engine by hiring writers for $50.00 an article to write lengthy blogs that say a whole lot of nothing.

You should still blog. Don't blog with the purpose of becoming a famous professional blogger. In the context of landing a job offer in five days, you don't even have to write about your profession. You can write about your passions and things that interest you. You can write about the personal goals you're setting and the progress you've made, whether it's running a marathon or reading one book a week.

When an employer reads your blog before giving you an interview, they get to know you on a personal level. They learn about your beliefs and values. They discover who you are as a person outside of your professional life, which can't be found on your resume. By the time you're both in the interview, the employer can go beyond the basic, superficial questions and ask you deeper questions about the things they read on your blog. And if you both have shared interests and values, it's like there is an unspoken understanding before you open your mouth.

Employers don't hire the most qualified and capable job candidate. They hire someone who is good enough to do the job and that they can talk to. Work is more enjoyable when you work with other people you trust and can talk to about things that aren't work-related. A job would be boring if all you talked about was work. This is why the less qualified candidate gets hired.

Seven years ago, there was an elderly lady who wanted me to do bookkeeping for her rental properties. At the time, I didn't go to college yet. When she found out I didn't go to college, she said I was unqualified to do the work. I kept in touch with her (she's like a grandma to me) and this past summer, I visited her. I told her I do real estate accounting and bookkeeping now as a full-time job, and I own a company too. She still didn't consider me "qualified" because I didn't major in accounting in school. I didn't take a single accounting class in college. My accounting skills were completely self-taught. She wanted to use people who had formal qualifications.

Finally, last week, while I was in the middle of writing this book, she called me asking if I wanted to take on the work. She told me she couldn't handle working with all the other bookkeepers she hired in the past. She couldn't have a conversation with any of them. I was the only person able to hold a deep conversation with her. I accepted.

I felt the same way when I was hiring my team. If I'm going to work with someone intimately, I need to get to know them as a person so we can build trust and understand each other. My team knows I eventually want Annie Yang Financial Corporation to make a billion dollars. Without a lot of trust, it would never happen.

Making YouTube Videos

I know some of you are shy. If you're not comfortable being in front of the camera, you can always go the podcast route. I don't have a podcast so I can't say much about it, so I'm going to explain this from the perspective of a YouTuber.

Even if you're a complete beginner in your industry and you're working an entry-level job, you can still use YouTube to build your authority. Read books within your industry and make book summary and book review videos.

If you want to go the extra mile, you can contact the author and ask for a recorded interview and post the interview. Not every author will agree to an interview. You need to be persistent and constantly follow up. Soon enough, with enough interviews posted online, people will see you as an expert, simply because you've associated yourself with experts. This is also a brilliant strategy because you naturally make connections, while also advertising the author. It's a win-win for everyone.

Don't ask these authors for anything in return. Successful people guard themselves because everyone wants something these days. Genuinely cultivate your relationships with these people and become friends. Only later, when you really need something, ask to tap into their network. Give more than you take.

Writing A Book

Many people think writing a book is a huge deal. In the past, publishing companies acted as the gatekeeper. Publishing companies didn't want to publish your book unless they knew your book would be profitable. They had to print thousands of copies of your book to keep the cost of printing low. Under that context, in the past, becoming an author was a huge accomplishment.

Amazon has turned the book publishing and retail industry upside down. Amazon is the world's largest bookstore today. Amazon's Kindle Publishing allows anyone to write and publish a book. It is now affordable to print copies of a book on demand, so books only get printed after they are sold.

Many people feel unqualified to write a book. That couldn't be further from the truth. I attended the Small Business Expo in New York City and listened to a sales pitch for a seminar called *Publish A Book and Grow Rich*. The salesperson had developed a system to write and publish a book in only 40 hours, and he said if we bought now, it would only cost $97.00 to attend the seminar and we could bring a friend for free. I turned to the stranger next to me and asked if she was interested. She was, so I registered for the seminar and asked her to pay me $48.50.

It was the best $48.50 I ever spent.

At the seminar, the trainer let us in on a secret: most books sell under 2,000 copies. If you earn $10.00 from every book, that's $20,000.00 from book sales. That's like working full-time for one year, earning minimum wage. The vast majority of authors don't get rich from writing a book. Instead, they get rich from the opportunities that come with being able to call themselves an author.

The opportunities come in the form of better job offers, speaking engagements, getting interviewed on TV, etc.

At 22 years old, I wrote and published *1001 Ways to Save Money* from start to finish in only 3 months. Aside from the few friends and family that pre-ordered my book, the book made zero sales for 3 years. But the book gave me an edge over the competition during my job searches because I stood out. Everyone has a bachelor's degree these days. Rarely does a hiring manager or recruiter come across an author. That was enough to make them curious to learn more about me. People believed that because I gained the title of author, I must be an expert or that at the very least, I must have a lot of discipline to sit down and finish writing a book— both outstanding qualities for an employee.

After my YouTube channel took off, I started promoting my book at the end of every video, asking people to buy my book and leave a review because I don't accept sponsorships. And my fans showed me their support. A loyal fan told me that *The Life-Changing Magic of Tidying Up* by Marie Kondo and *1001 Ways to Save Money* by yours truly were her two favorite books of all time. I was deeply touched knowing I changed people's lives through the power of the written word.

After I got over 100 reviews, someone from the Brooklyn College CollegeNow program reached out to me. She was inspired by my story of how I didn't go straight to college. She loved my book and believed young people needed to read it. She invited me to give a speech at Brooklyn College and I accepted. That was my first professional speaking gig. So now I can add professional public speaker to my bio.

Basically, a book project that took me only 3 months to finish ended up being more impressive than a bachelor's degree that typically takes 4 years to finish. The book changed the trajectory of my life.

Enough about me.

Have you changed your mind about writing a book?

How can you write your first book?

Here's the system.

Buy a pack of index cards and cut them in half (you can buy two packs, but I buy one pack and cut them in half to save money).

Brainstorm 10 subjects you know a lot about and write each subject on one index card.

Now decide on the one subject that people really want to buy and read. If you can't narrow it down to one, pick one and tell yourself you can always write a 2nd or 3rd book later. Your goal is to write your 1st book.

Brainstorm 10 main ideas or themes you want the reader to know about this subject and write each one on an index card. Reorder the index cards in an order that makes the most sense. This will be your table of contents.

For each chapter of your book, brainstorm ten questions the reader would have about that idea.

With ten chapters and ten questions each, you should have 100 questions. Reorder the questions within each chapter.

For each question, brainstorm three examples that would help you convey your point or your answer.

Now you're done.

You just need to type up your book outline into Microsoft Word.

It should look something like this:

Book Title by Your Name Here
- Main Idea #1 (Chapter #1)
  - Question #1
    - Example #1
    - Example #2
    - Example #3
  - Question #2
    - Example #1
    - Example #2
    - Example #3

- o Question #3
  - ▪ Example #1
  - ▪ Example #2
  - ▪ Example #3
- o Etc…
- Main Idea #2 (Chapter #2)
  - o Question #1
    - ▪ Example #1
    - ▪ Example #2
    - ▪ Example #3
  - o Question #2
    - ▪ Example #1
    - ▪ Example #2
    - ▪ Example #3
  - o Etc…

Spend one hour per day reading the questions out loud for one chapter and answering the questions using the voice memo app on your smartphone. If you're stuck on how to answer the question, that's where research comes in to save the day. Research the topic and rephrase the answer in your own words.

After ten days, you should have ten hours of recording. Upload your recordings into a program called Descript (Descript.com/transcription), which will transcribe your audio for only $12.00. It's a $12/month subscription for ten hours of transcription per month—remember to cancel your subscription… I forgot to cancel mine.

You're now ten hours into this project and your first draft is done. It's time to edit the manuscript. You don't need to hire a professional editor. For *1001 Ways to Save Money*, I paid for a 3-month Grammarly Premium subscription and used a website called HemingwayApp.com. If you edit one chapter per week, you'll finish editing in ten weeks.

Finally, you turn your manuscript into a book.

Hire a graphic designer to design the cover of your book. The cover sells the book. You can check out 99designs.com for book cover designers. Expect to pay between $350.00 and $900.00 for a book cover. Don't do it yourself. Don't cheap out on this. Readers can spot an amateur job from a mile away.

Hire a copywriter to write your blurb. You can either use Fiverr (I used that for my 1st edition) or use Polgarus Studio (I used them for my 2nd edition). Every copywriter will ask you to summarize your book or ask you to write your own blurb and then they will improve your blurb. Polgarus Studio charges more money, but they will actually read your entire manuscript and handpick the best parts of your book for the back cover copy.

Buy an interior book design template from <u>BookDesignTemplates.com</u> for $59.00 and use their Microsoft Word Template to format your book. Their templates come with instructions.

Now it's just a matter of uploading your book to Kindle Publishing. There are already many YouTube videos and articles on how to do this. If you're a Millennial, it should be easy for you to figure this part out.

Approximately 72 hours after you finish submitting your information and files to Kindle Publishing, your book will be on Amazon, ready for sale.

You can now call yourself an author.

Congratulations!

Chapter 24

Being Fabulous in Everything You Do

Whatever you do, be fabulous doing it. You need to be outstanding in order to stand out from the crowd. I got this idea from Ellen Lubin-Sherman's book, *The Essentials of Fabulous*. Being fabulous has nothing to do with your physical appearance. It has everything to do with how you present yourself to the world. From now on, be fabulous.

Being fabulous is about the little things, like the way you say hello and smile at people, the way you say "great morning!" instead of "good morning...," the way you answer when asked "how are you?" ("today is the best day of my life, because all I have is today"), the way you give people thank you cards, the way you always show up to someone's house with a small gift, the way you go out of your way to make and drop off chicken noodle soup for a sick friend, the way you put your phone away whenever you're having a conversation with someone, the way you leave cheerful voicemails.

It could be doing small things for a coworker having a bad day at work (you can tell from the door slamming or the sighing), like heading over to Dunkin' Donuts across the street to buy a $2.00 donut for her. Leaving it on her desk when she goes to the bathroom, so that when she comes back, she will find this sweet surprise!

It could be writing affirmations on post-it notes and leaving them on your colleague's cubicle walls so whenever she's feeling negative, she can look up and see the affirmations and remind herself that everything will be okay.

It could be repairing your boss's worn leather chair with leather repair tape when he's away on vacation. When he comes back and sits in his chair, he'll realize the armrests are nice and smooth again.

It could be hearing from a mutual friend about an acquaintance you only met once, who is struggling with a certain problem, so you mail that acquaintance a gift-wrapped book with ideas on how to solve that problem.

When you practice the art of being fabulous, people remember how you made them feel. People will forget what you said or did, but they will never forget how you made them feel.

Chapter 25

Presenting Your Best Self in Every Situation

Regardless of your age, you must always put an effort into looking your best wherever you go. Looking your best is about taking the body you've been born with and maxing out your beauty to its fullest potential. This means losing the weight if you need to, eating healthy food, exercising, getting an adequate amount of sleep every night, wearing clothes that flatter you, getting a nice haircut, waxing your eyebrows, wearing perfume/cologne, and if you're a woman, wearing makeup and painting your nails.

I used to think judging people based on their physical appearance was superficial. I refused to spend my money on improving my appearance. I believed someone's character and personality were more important than what they looked like on the outside and that other people should think the same way. One day, I listened to a Jim Rohn recording where he said that before you open your mouth to speak, people are going to take a look. You can't spend your life wishing that people would stop judging you by your appearance. You'll just be frustrated. You need to accept the reality.

When you dress your best everywhere you go, people will want to introduce you to everyone they know. If you dress like a slob, you communicate that you can't even take care of your personal affairs, let alone work-related matters. Who wants to introduce that kind of person?

Imagine you work at a company that serves high-profile clients. You're working in an entry-level position that doesn't have a lot of responsibility and doesn't require interacting with clients. You're allowed to wear whatever you want at this job. But it's not enough to just produce stellar work. You want to dress so well that your boss will show you off to every supervisor and client he knows, because you represent him. You should dress for the job you want, not the job you already have—every single day.

The same concept applies to marriage. As I'm writing this, my husband is in Japan for a year, doing his PhD research. I told him I'm going to practice doing my makeup every single day so that when I visit him in Japan, I'll look so beautiful he won't recognize me at the airport. He will go around introducing me to everyone he knows in Japan, proudly announcing, "Everyone, this is my trophy wife, Annie Yang." He chuckled when I told him this, but I am serious.

I hired a professional image consultant of 35 years, Ginger Burr from Total Image Consultants (TotalImageConsultants.com), to help me create the right image. I paid Ginger $3,000.00 for private coaching (I spread it out into monthly payments of approximately $250.00 and worked it into my budget). Every time I wanted to buy a new piece of clothing, I would take a picture of myself wearing it and email it to Ginger for advice on whether it looked good or bad on me, and whether I should buy it. She would explain why it looked that way on my body specifically. With time, I learned certain necklines looked great on me while others made my shoulders look too broad. I learned how different shapes looked on my body type. I learned little details, like I should wear blazers that don't have pocket flaps because I have such a small body frame. And if a blazer already has pocket flaps, I can go to a tailor to get them removed. She also taught me how to style a certain piece with shoes and accessories so I could complete the outfit.

I felt ashamed to publicly say that I was paying someone to help me with my wardrobe because I felt like people were going to judge me for not even knowing how to dress myself properly as an adult. It seemed like something other women just intuitively knew how to do. I felt even worse since I have a YouTube channel and book that tells people not to waste their money on things like this, but I fully changed my mind. The $3,000.00 I spent on Ginger's advice was 100% worth it. After I started working with her, I stopped wasting money on clothes that looked okay but not great on me, and I started receiving compliments from strangers everywhere I went. And the price I paid was a one-time thing. I know exactly what looks great on me without having to ask Ginger anymore.

I don't regret spending the $3,000.00, but I know I can't recommend everyone to do the same. Other people might not have room in their budget to spend $250.00 a month on an image consultant, plus a new wardrobe budget. I think the best value you get for your money is the personal color analysis and fashion fit formula.

The personal color analysis is a service where an image consultant puts together a color palette that will always look the best on you. There is no such thing as one red. Red could be bright, light, dark, muted, toasted, tinted, warm, or cool. The image consultant puts 2,000 color swatches against your face and hand picks only the best shades of each color that will make your skin vibrant. All the colors in your color palette look great together, so you don't have to worry about whether the color of your shirt will go well with the color of your pants. The color palette also saves a lot of time when shopping because you'll walk into a store and quickly eliminate all the clothes that won't look good on you just by glancing at the colors on a rack.

The fashion fit formula is a system based on the vertical measurements of your body. You can use it to tailor your clothes to look the most flattering on you. Have you ever noticed just how effortlessly polished a celebrity looks in a white shirt and blue jeans? It's not an accident. You can upgrade the white shirt and blue jeans look with good tailoring. When you buy clothes off the rack, the designer designed those clothes for models of a certain height. It could be 5 feet 6 inches tall... it could be 6 feet tall. Your clothes can fit you fine width wise, but vertically, you're wearing clothes that were designed for someone else. You need to hem all your clothes to a certain part of your body to look vertically balanced. For example, my short sleeves should always hit 2 inches above my elbow, my ¾ sleeves should always hit 1 inch below my elbow, my belts should always be 1 to 1 ½ inches wide, short jackets should always hit 32 inches above the floor without shoes on, etc. After I started tailoring everything, I felt like anything that wasn't tailored to my fashion fit formula looked frumpy. Tailoring my clothes improved my self-confidence because now I look great everywhere I go.

Chapter 26

Enhancing Virtual Meetings With Realistic and Stylish Zoom Backgrounds

Since we do more business in video conference calls these days, you need to up your game in this department. While I live in a home that's nicely decorated, it's not nicely decorated for videography. It's incredibly difficult to design a space that looks great on video and meets the practical needs of maximizing my workspace.

I solved this problem by buying a collapsible green screen from Amazon for $200.00. In ten seconds, I pull the green screen up. In ten seconds, I fold it back down. Then I store the green screen under my bed.

I found that a webcam and lighting matter a lot in making a green screen background look more real. A high-quality HD or 4K webcam makes it so that your face looks just as sharp and crisp as the fake background. A ring light shining on your face makes it so that the direction of the light source matches. If you don't do both, the video looks fake, even if you have a green screen.

For my background, I downloaded 200 realistic-looking Zoom backgrounds I found on the Internet, and I took screenshots of myself in front of all 200 backgrounds. I sent them to my graphic designer, Luis, and told him to pick the one that best conveyed my branding and reputation. I asked him to Photoshop the lighting in the picture to match the lighting in my room so that it looked even more real. He even went as far as blurring the plant in my background because objects that are farther away shouldn't look that sharp.

The last thing to adjust is the height of your camera. If you're using a laptop, prop your laptop up with a book to make it higher. The camera should be eye level—if angled too low, people will see more of your chin and nostrils. The top of your head should have a little space between your hair and the top edge of the video frame.

Chapter 27

Adapting and Thriving in a Rapidly Changing World

In a poor economy, it's still possible to land a job offer in five days. When money is scarce and companies don't want to spend, work still needs to be done. Companies become pickier with how they spend their money. The money always ends up getting spent on the cream of the crop, which is why you see the people making all the money continuing to make even more money. It's not like all job opportunities are gone in a poor economy. The opportunities still exist—it's simply more difficult for the average job applicant because those opportunities keep getting awarded to the same top five percent of job applicants. More work goes to *less* people and to the *best* people.

There is no shortcut to becoming the best. The only way is to spend one hour per day for the rest of your life continuing your education from a variety of sources. You know, I've found it helpful to have a well-structured, adaptable plan to guide my ongoing learning and keep my professional skills sharpened. This has been such a game changer for me, and I want to share it with you too. Pop over to annieyangfinancial.com/learning-plan and download the Rising to the Top: Your Adaptable Personal Development Plan. It's a resource I've put together to help folks like you and me stay on track in our self-education journey.

I often think about Stephen Covey's example of sharpening the saw. Give two people the task of chopping down a tree. The first person spends all six hours trying to chop down the tree and doesn't accomplish anything. The second person spends the first four hours sharpening the saw, and the last two hours quickly chopping down the tree.

Everyone graduates college with more or less the same knowledge and expertise (an even playing field). After ten years, some rise to the top of the industry (or are on the way to the top), some stay average, and some work jobs that don't require a degree. The latter are better off not having gone to college to begin with.

The difference is in sharpening the saw daily. You must sharpen your mind.

Ten years after graduating college, the knowledge you learned will have depreciated in value because it will no longer be relevant in our rapidly changing world. You need to continue learning new things daily.

The dictionary definition of intelligence is "the ability to acquire and apply knowledge and skills." Not only must you absorb new information like a sponge, but you must also proactively apply new knowledge in any project or endeavor you're trying to accomplish.

From this day forward, carry a notebook with you everywhere you go. Write down what you learned. Take notes of everything.

Mark Zuckerberg gave a speech to entrepreneurs in Silicon Valley on the lessons he learned from creating Facebook and his perspective of the Internet industry. Only two people in the audience were taking notes and those two people were also the most successful people in the room.

I recently had a similar experience at a piano seminar. I'm learning classical piano, and I found out New England Conservatory offers free seminars on Fridays that are open to the public. I've been attending the seminars so that I can take full advantage of the free world-class music education to further my piano studies. The first seminar I attended was taught by a famous piano duo. They gave a bunch of secrets about how they used social media to build their career and fanbase. The information they gave was gold. I read a lot about sales and marketing, and you cannot find this kind of information on the Internet. I took pages of notes at that seminar.

Most of the attendees at the seminar were students enrolled at New England Conservatory, shelling out $53,000.00 per year in tuition. During the seminar, I looked around the room and 80% of the attendees were on their phones texting or playing video games. They might as well have just stayed home. The remaining 20% that were paying attention did not take notes. Statistically, we retain 50% of the information immediately after a presentation. The next day, we remember 25%. The next week, we remember only 10%. Because of this statistic, I guarantee you only 1% of the people (I am the 1%) at that seminar will apply everything that was taught. I believe this is why so few succeed.

Chapter 28

Mastering Public Speaking to Answer Tough Interview Questions

Warren Buffett said that the easiest way to improve your value by 50% is to learn public speaking. That billionaire is right! I learned public speaking after I read that article.

Public speaking is ranked the #1 fear by the majority of people. Death is ranked #2. People are more afraid to give a eulogy than to die.

Public speaking is a skill you can develop. The only reason most people don't work on it is because they get emotionally hung up. If you're getting emotional thinking that you could never learn how to speak in public, ask yourself:

Do you get emotionally hung up about learning how to bake a cake?

What about learning how to drive?

What about learning to snowboard?

Those things don't conjure up the same fear, even though they are learnable skills. Your fear may be because the teacher picked on you to answer a question in class as a kid and you gave the wrong answer. Everyone looked at you weird and you forever felt the anxiety. You're not a kid anymore. Let it go. Adult audiences are not as immature.

The best way to improve at public speaking is to join Toastmasters International. You can go to <u>Toastmasters.org/find-a-club</u> and find a local club. Be a guest at different clubs first to get a good feel for which one you want to join. The membership fee is only $90.00 per year. It's cheaper than a Planet Fitness gym membership.

After you join Toastmasters, commit to giving ten speeches at a rate of at least one speech per month. In my experience (from watching newbies), those were the speakers who progressed the fastest. Anyone who spoke less than once a month might as well not have shown up. Once you get feedback on your speech, you can work on your next speech right away and implement the feedback. You gain momentum when you do it often enough. I watched shy people go from being nervous in their first speech, to being confident by their 10th speech. By their 20th speech, they could command a room. It was like watching a caterpillar transform into a butterfly.

Record all your speeches. People who improve the most record their speeches and watch it afterwards. It's a painful experience and I hated doing it. But it's the only way to get better. You can't tell if you successfully implemented your previous feedback unless you look. You also need to learn to critique yourself for improvement because you won't always have other people to give you feedback. If you fixed three things in your speech after your first one, then after ten speeches, you'll have fixed 27 things. The difference between the first and tenth speech will be night and day.

The same concept applies to everything you do—not just public speaking. For my YouTube videos, when I first started, they weren't that good. To get better at making them, I would watch my latest video, and after giving myself feedback, I would improve on three things for my next video. Then in the next video, I would improve on three more things. I kept doing that and after 50 videos, I've come a long way in the quality of my content.

Beyond public speaking, you should join Toastmasters because in every meeting, they do Table Topics. The Table Topics Master picks a random person, who then has to walk to the front of the room and answer a random question. The person answering has to speak for at least 60 seconds for the answer to be valid.

Table Topics is a valuable exercise. It teaches you how to think on your feet. Too many people try to prepare for an interview by checking GlassDoor.com to see what kind of questions the interviewer will ask. There are even job-hunting books that will list the most common interview questions and teach you the "right" answer. You might feel you're prepared, but that's a false sense of confidence. If you follow the advice from those job-hunting books and articles, you'll end up giving scripted answers that the interviewer has heard a million times. And (innocently) worse, you'll end up telling the interviewer what you think she wants to hear, rather than telling her what you really think. This is terrible because you'll be hired based on false notions, and then after you're hired, both you and the company will wonder why you're not a good cultural fit. You need to learn how to speak authentically and how to maintain your composure under pressure, and the only way to achieve this is by practicing it every single week for a year. That way, acing interviews will be a piece of cake.

Chapter 29

Improving Your Voice for Increased Competence and Credibility

Improve your voice. If you listen, you'll find that many people mumble or don't enunciate words. It always causes me to say, "Huh? What did you say? Can you repeat that?" After a while, I don't want to seem rude, so I nod my head and pretend I understand, and hope I guess the core message correctly from the context of the words.

Just because you are born in an English-speaking country and English is your native language doesn't automatically make you articulate. Your goal should be to sound like a news anchor on TV with a standard accent. When you speak with a standard accent, people judge you as more intelligent, competent, and credible.

There isn't one specific online course that contains all the information on how to speak more articulately. I learned vocal articulation in a community college class and from Roger Love's *Vocal Power: Speaking with Authority, Clarity, and Conviction* and *Set Your Voice Free: How To Get The Singing Or Speaking Voice You Want.*

In addition to checking out Roger Love's resources, you should be able to find more vocal articulation exercises online to improve your speaking voice. You can also do tongue twisters slowly. Always look up the pronunciation of words you're not sure about, even for commonly spoken words. There is no faster way to sound stupid than to pronounce a word incorrectly. I also recommend reading one page from a book out loud every day and recording yourself. Listen to your recording and fix the little details in your voice. With time, your voice will sound different.

If you need extra help, you can hire a voice coach. I was already articulate from doing everything I mentioned above, but there was something that annoyed me about the way I spoke, and I couldn't put my finger on it. I hired Janelle Winston from the SpeechCoach Company (SpeechCoachCompany.com) to help me. She pointed out that when I was nervous, I would raise the inflection at the end of a sentence, which made my statement sound like a question. That was a bad habit and it made me sound like I was unsure of myself. After I became aware of this, I fixed it.

Chapter 30

Avoiding Common Email Pitfalls in Professional Communication

Email communication is usually an afterthought, but this is a skill you can learn. Ever emailed someone by accident before you meant to click send? Or forgotten your attachment? A short book you can read about all the mistakes people make when writing an email, and the trick to avoiding them is *33 Ways Not to Screw Up Your Business Emails* by Anne Janzer.

Chapter 31

Staying Organized to Boost Your Professional Image

How organized you are affects people's perception. Would you trust your tax accountant to process your tax return properly if they were disorganized? I asked a friend, also a long-time business owner, for advice on how I can get ahead in my career. He told me to organize everything. Organize my room, organize my desk, organize my wardrobe, organize my finances, organize my contacts list, organize my folders and files on my computer, organize my email inbox, organize my calendar, basically organize my entire life. I didn't understand the importance, but I followed his advice.

During a job interview, I asked what caused the job opening—basically, why did the previous person leave? They fired her for a variety of reasons, but one complaint was that she was disorganized. Her desk was always a mess. After they hired me, I made sure to keep the desk organized. People would comment about how I was so much more organized than the last person. They were always concerned when putting something on her desk for fear of it getting lost. They really loved working with me.

Chapter 32

Better Managing Your Time for Increased Productivity

"Waking up this morning, I smile. Twenty-four brand new hours are before me. I vow to live fully in each moment and to look at all beings with eyes of compassion."

— Thich Nhat Hanh

Time management is, in fact, self-management from a time perspective. As you explore various time management systems and test them out, you will discover that the biggest obstacle to managing your time effectively is yourself. It's easy to add items to our calendars, but we often choose not to consult them or follow through with the tasks listed. This behavior can be a major hindrance to achieving our dreams.

We tend to be more diligent in keeping commitments we make to others than those we make solely to ourselves. By doing so, we prioritize others over ourselves. This can result in feelings of self-disappointment. To overcome this, we must honor every commitment we make. Failing to follow our calendar sends a message that we are incapable or unworthy of the tasks we set for ourselves. To combat this, we must consistently show up when we say we will, no matter how unworthy we may feel.

Transitioning to the practical aspect of time management, experiment with different calendars and time management systems to determine what works best for your current stage in life. In the past, I found it helpful to schedule every single activity, no matter how minor, in my calendar. However, if I were to do the same today, it would feel overly restrictive, as I would feel compelled to follow my calendar schedule to the letter. While I still use a calendar for events, I now also rely on Basecamp, a project and task management software, to track deadlines separately and display them in order of priority. This system offers greater flexibility when adjustments are needed.

Chapter 33

Doubling Your Productivity by Increasing Typing Speed

Touch typing is a skill that everyone, especially those working in an office, could improve on. The average person types only 42 words per minute. If you can type twice as fast at 85 words per minute, you'll be twice as productive in computer-related work. A side benefit of typing fast with few mistakes is that people will think you're highly competent at what you're doing, even when you're not.

You should learn to type with ten fingers slowly, then increase your speed with practice. First, focus on accuracy and on retraining muscle memory, and then focus on getting faster. TypingStudy.com is an excellent website for teaching you which finger should type which key. After you learn that, you can use Keybr.com for daily practice.

Don't lose patience—it takes a long time to get better. I paid my two employees to learn and practice touch typing daily for half an hour. They spent the first three months relearning where to place their fingers. One of them was secretly cursing me in her head. She didn't see the point because she was typing slower. But now that she types more efficiently, she sees the benefits and agrees with me. This is an important skill to learn if you want to be a more productive worker.

Chapter 34

Identifying and Addressing Skill Gaps for Career Advancement

Create a list of hard or technical skills you are missing. Lacking them prevents you from getting promoted. Employers constantly complain that they can't find people with the right skills. You can identify a list of skills that employers want and fix this problem by learning them all.

In Chapter 18: Optimizing Your LinkedIn Profile To Maximize Interview Requests, you compiled a list of skills that other people on LinkedIn already had for the job title you want. Based on that list, create a new list of the skills you're missing.

While you're compiling this list, go to annieyangfinancial.com/skill-gaps and download two incredibly practical resources: the Personal SWOT Analysis for Career Advancement and the Skill Gap Analysis Worksheet. These tools will not only aid you in identifying the skills you're currently lacking but also give you a broader view of your professional strengths and weaknesses. This can set you up for a more strategic approach to your career growth.

Search job boards for the job listings with your desired title. Look at the qualifications listed and add them to your list. Job seekers complain employers demand too many qualifications from candidates. The worst time to improve your skill set is when you're looking for a new job because you feel like life isn't under control. You should improve your skill set to match what today's employers want, so when it's time for you to apply for a new job, your application will go to the top of the pile.

Also, check out a website called PayScale.com. PayScale will ask you for your current job title, skill set, and salary, and give you recommendations on skills you should learn that will help you make more money.

Chapter 35

Mastering Office Software: Becoming the Go-To Resource for Technical Expertise

Many companies will buy software for a handful of its features. They buy a software because they see other companies in the same industry using it, or someone recommended it, or maybe a salesperson promised it would solve their problem. The owner or the manager never takes the time to learn about every single thing the software can do. It's possible that they have three different software when one software could already do what the other two did. Companies do not maximize the full value of their purchase.

If you work in an office, compile a list of all the software that is being used. Add this to your list of skills you need to learn. In your free time at work, read every article, watch every video, and sign up for every live webinar or demo that you can find about how to use the software. The software's documentation is a good place to start. You can later watch YouTube videos of how other companies adapted the software to fit their needs. This will give you more ideas on how the company you work for can use the software. Remember to take notes.

When you are done, go to your manager and explain the useful features the company isn't already using. Then offer to implement those new features and teach the rest of the team how to use it. Do this for every single piece of software the company uses. You will end up being the go-to expert whenever a colleague is struggling with software, and you will become known as the star employee who helps the company run more efficiently.

You'll find this strategy to be valuable because if your company struggled with the software, chances are, all the companies in your industry struggled with the same software. When it's time for your next job interview, you'll be able to list a bunch of things your future employer could do to improve the entire operation. The hiring manager will want to give you a job offer right away before a competitor snatches you up.

Chapter 36

Documenting and Showcasing
Your Achievements

Add value at your current job so you can be ready to talk about achievements and accomplishments (at your current company) when you are at an interview. Too many people lie or sugarcoat their story to make themselves look more competent and important. Interviewers can see right through the bullshit when they press you for details.

One candidate I interviewed said that one of the hardest problems he ever solved was creating a nonprofit that helped orphans living in the slums of Nairobi. He said he raised money to buy food and clothes for 200 children. When I pressed for details on exactly how he achieved that, he said that he and a group of friends had set up a page on social media and asked people to donate. They got donations, and then handed the money to the people who needed it. When I asked whether it was a one-time thing or a continuing thing, he said it was a one-time thing. When I asked how they helped besides collecting money (anyone can collect money... it's not a hard thing to do), he said he didn't help in any other way. Then when I asked him how the recipients were doing today, he said he never followed up. So much for the impressive "I started a nonprofit" story that got him the interview.

You need to have real accomplishments that actually matter. When an interviewer like me is grilling you for details, you should be able to answer easily.

To create real accomplishments in the workplace, you need to proactively uncover real problems. Take the time and be curious to learn exactly what are the obstacles holding the company back from growing or running more efficiently.

A good place to start is complaints. People like to avoid complaints and think that if they ignore something long enough, the problem will go away. Complaints don't exist in a vacuum. Every complaint is a sign that a problem exists. Write the complaint down in your notebook and start thinking about how you can solve the problem. Those problems are your opportunity to make more money. When you view problems as opportunities, you'll discover that there is no shortage of problems and therefore, no shortage of opportunities. It is problem solving that pays good money because you've made their life so much better.

Another way to identify problems is to go to your boss and ask your boss why your job even exists. What problem did they think they would solve by creating the position and hiring somebody? Why are you on the payroll? Employees often think they were hired to do a set of tasks. No, your boss created the set of tasks in hopes of solving a specific problem. Get clear on the problem and look for ways to improve how the job is done.

Lastly, conduct a 360-degree analysis of everything that is wrong with the company. Talk to every single client, vendor, and employee and ask them what things annoy them about the company or how they wish the company operated. Write everything down in your notebook. After a while, you'll find trends. Go to your boss with your list and tell your boss you've identified all these problems in the company that's holding the company back, and that you would like to work on some of these problems. Ask your boss for which one you should tackle first and then one by one, solve all of them. Shortly, you'll have a lot of accomplishments under your belt.

Develop an ownership mindset. Take ownership of all the company's problems as if you owned the company. Employees often see problems as, "That's not my job," or "That's not my problem." It's selfish. When you take ownership of the company's problems, you will be seen and respected as a real leader. The real leader isn't the one with the job title of a leader. I'm sure you've seen people in the workplace who had the job title of a leader, but no one respected or listened to them. The real leader in a company is the one who can influence everyone without force. You need to gain influence before you step into the leadership title.

Chapter 37

Raising Your Work Standards to Deliver Consistent High-Quality Results

You must produce excellent work if you want to get ahead. Everyone can learn how to do something, but not everyone can do it well. The reason isn't lack of ability, but lack of care for the final result.

I once hired two freelance video editors (they were partners) who worked with Fortune 500 companies that regularly advertised commercials on TV. I expected high-quality editing because I know for a fact that all TV commercials are meticulously edited frame by frame. For $250 per 12-minute video, they promised high-quality video editing.

The quality of their editing was so bad, it was laughable. It was embarrassing because I edited my own videos better than they did and no one ever paid me to edit videos. If the standard to become a professional was really that low, I could make a good living editing videos for other people.

In one video, I was showing my audience the notes in my notebook. The left side had notes written all over the page, and the right side was blank. Anyone looking at it would know immediately that putting text on top of the video required positioning it on the right side, so that people could read the notes on the left side. I even noted these instructions when I assigned the project.

But the editors covered the side of the notebook that had notes on it—not once, but at least 10 times in that video. They didn't follow instructions.

When they added text (in another video), they would make it 10pt font, then 18pt font, then 24pt font. There was no consistency in font size. It was like a middle schooler had edited it.

The audio was also bad. My voice would go from extremely loud to extremely quiet. It hurt my ears to watch my video because I kept having to adjust the volume of my speakers.

When I complained about the quality of the work, they made their assistant talk to me instead of calling me themselves. The assistant relayed I was too picky and demanding. Apparently, they spent over 40 hours editing one 10-minute video and were getting paid less than minimum wage at that point. There was no way it took that long—I edited all my videos for several years. A 10-minute video would take me five hours to edit. The $250 flat rate would have easily translated to $50/hour if I had to do it myself. The hourly rate would have been even higher for them because I wasn't familiar with all the keyboard shortcuts inside Adobe Premier Pro.

The assistant said that when they accepted my video editing projects, they thought that since my videos were supposed to be made for YouTube and not for TV, it would be "low effort" and a good way for them to "make a quick and easy buck." They never intended to put much effort into the editing to begin with. That explained why their final videos looked like they didn't even watch the videos from beginning to end before sending them back to me. They didn't deliver excellence because they didn't care.

If you can consistently deliver excellent work, you already stand out from the crowd. There is very little competition because most people just want to deliver OK quality work and move on.

Chapter 38

Taking on Additional Responsibilities to Gain Trust and Recognition

Whenever you're assigned a task, finish the task quickly, and ask for more responsibility. Don't use the free time to mess around and do whatever you want. At first, your boss isn't going to trust you. Your boss is going to give you minor tasks. Keep finishing the tasks quickly and asking for more responsibility. Soon enough, your boss will run out of minor tasks to assign and will have to assign big, important tasks.

Many employees take on more responsibility than they were originally hired to do, but their salary remains the same. Don't complain about your salary. The experience is worth far more than your current salary. When you apply for new jobs, you will talk about all the different things you did for your current company, and you'll have a nice pay bump. Delay your gratification.

Chapter 39

Embracing Constructive Feedback With a Positive Attitude

Don't get offended or defensive when people give you unsolicited feedback. It opens the opportunity for you to improve. The next time someone offers unsolicited feedback, reply, "Thank you so much for your advice. I really appreciate it."

Write down the unsolicited feedback in your notebook. Think about where this advice is coming from. It is usually from personal experience. Chances are high that you have a blind spot in an area that you didn't even know existed. The worst thing in life is not knowing what you don't know. You will succeed much faster when you learn from other people's experiences. You don't have to make the same mistakes.

Work on improving in this area, and then go back to the same person and say, "I took some time to fix what you told me. I've done x, y, and z to improve in this area. This is the result I am getting. This is the obstacle I am facing. Can I get new feedback and any ideas on how I can improve further?" Write it down in your notebook again and work on improving in that area.

Most people will stop giving unsolicited feedback if you react negatively. If you show people you can handle feedback well, they'll point out even more blind spots for you, so you can work on them in the future. Don't surround yourself with yes men who tell you how great you are. Surround yourself with people who aren't afraid to tell you the reality or tell you you're wrong.

Chapter 40

Learning From Successful People and Applying Their Strategies

Success doesn't happen by accident, nor is it a bit of luck. Whenever we see someone successful, we discount their accomplishments by saying they merely got lucky. It's an easy way to make yourself feel better about how your own life turned out.

Yes, luck played a role. But if that successful person spent her evenings watching Netflix all night instead of honing her craft and constantly planning, learning, and networking, would she be where she is today?

The next time you look at successful people doing what you want to do, stop downplaying their hard work. Psychologically, your mind will never allow you to become the thing you hate. If you hate rich and successful people, you will never become rich and successful because you'll hate yourself. You would end up self-sabotaging every step of the way to protect yourself.

Once you catch your thoughts, change your mindset to, "Amazing! If this person can do it, I can do it too. If it's been done before by someone else, it's living proof that my dream is reasonable and doable. I wonder how they got there. What can I learn from this person? Let me read about them so I can follow in their footsteps."

Chapter 41

Transforming Past Job Experiences Into Compelling Stories

You can't change your past, but you can change how you look at it. You need to talk about your previous jobs in the interview, and even if you didn't accomplish anything major, you can still use those experiences in your favor. It's about changing your perspective and communicating it. At every single job, even menial minimum wage jobs, I'm sure you learned something valuable. If you're able to reflect deeply on your experiences, you'll have a lot of things to talk about in your interview.

This reflection is different for everyone, so I can't give any solid advice. For inspiration, I am sharing my past job experiences and the life lessons I learned from all of them.

To aid in your reflection, consider downloading Storytelling Mastery: Turning Job Experiences into Impactful Narratives, a guide complete with 200 inspirational words to enhance your narratives. Find it at annieyangfinancial.com/narratives.

Cashier at ShopRite

At ShopRite, the managers were always testing my scans per minute and complaining that I wasn't fast enough. I didn't have the PLU codes memorized and could never differentiate between parsley and cilantro, and cucumber and zucchini. I honestly thought I was a terrible cashier. After I submitted my resignation, the manager begged me to stay. I was shocked because he never praised me for doing a good job. According to the job metrics, I wasn't good at my job compared to the other cashiers.

It turns out I was extremely punctual and reliable. I always clocked in and out within 5 minutes of my shift and I never called in sick. I didn't know my coworkers had problems showing up to work on time. The reason I showed up on time was because I was getting paid only $8.00/hour and I wanted to get paid for every minute I could work. If I showed up 10 minutes late every day for 5 days, then in one week I would lose 50 minutes' worth of work. In one year, that's 43 hours of lost income. I assumed everyone showed up to work on time. The valuable lesson I learned at this job was that punctuality was far more important than the official job metrics.

Cashier at Florence Grocery Store

All the cashiers lived within a 5-minute walk from the grocery store, including me. One coworker lived across the street from the store (you could see him crossing the street through the store window), yet there was not a single day when he showed up on time. He couldn't use traffic as an excuse, so he always made up a different excuse. All my coworkers also liked to party the night before work, so they would wake up feeling hungover and call in sick. Every single week, it was a different coworker who called in sick, and my boss would ask me to cover someone's shift at least once a week.

My coworkers treated this job with little care and respect. They did the bare minimum. Their attitude was that if the job paid this little money, they would only put in this little effort. And if the job paid more money, then they would put in more effort.

At this job, I learned to develop a better attitude and not succumb to other people's work philosophy. Regardless of how much I was getting paid, I learned to always give my best at the job, and I practiced this mindset at work every day. I believed that everything at this job was preparation for the big day, for the once-in-a-lifetime opportunity in my faraway future. If you spend your entire life not doing your best work, then one day when you're handed a better opportunity, you won't do well because you never practiced giving your all.

Insider at Domino's Pizza

When I first started working at Domino's Pizza, I was angry with myself. All my life, everyone told me I had to go to college to be successful. I finally caved and went to college. At that point, I had just graduated from a community college with an associate degree, and I graduated from an online university with a bachelor's degree. So here I was. I finally had that piece of paper to my name. I could finally tick the college degree box that everyone said was so important.

I moved to Lubbock, TX (the middle of nowhere), a small city with very few good job opportunities. Employers there usually hired people recommended by someone they knew. Applying for jobs online didn't work out for me because there were only ten job listings in anything finance related. I also didn't know anyone since I just moved there. I also didn't drive, so I could only apply for jobs within walking distance. The only job I could get was at Domino's Pizza.

For weeks, all I did was complain to my husband about how low level this job was. I was on my feet all day (you weren't allowed to sit... there were no chairs for employees to sit), so my feet always hurt. And I came home smelling like pizza, so I had to wash my hair every day.

I stopped complaining after I met my blind coworker, Ricky Robles. He used to work as a sheriff. One morning, while driving to work, he pulled up to a stop sign, and suddenly, he couldn't see the stop sign. Doctors diagnosed him with glaucoma at 43 years old. After several operations, he finally lost his eyesight. He received disability income, but it paid less than half of what he used to make as a sheriff. He wanted to provide for his family and make his house payment. He wanted to prove to himself that he could still be a productive member of society, so he got a full-time job at Domino's Pizza folding boxes. He folded 3,000 pizza boxes a day for the last eleven years. He was genuinely grateful for the opportunity to work at Domino's Pizza and make an honest living.

Ricky's story taught me that there is no such thing as a job that is beneath me. Making pizza for customers was an honest way to earn money. Thousands of people got pizza delivered from our store because they needed a quick way to feed their families. We were creating happy memories for these families, especially the children. We were also saving time for busy adults who didn't have the time to cook after a long day at work. I learned that it's more important to focus on serving people than to focus on my pay.

Bookkeeper at Adventure Park

This was my second bookkeeping job. The first bookkeeping job was a couple of years prior, and my QuickBooks skills were rusty. A week before the first day of work, I borrowed Quick-Books for Dummies and Bookkeeping for Dummies from the library. I read through both books twice. Whenever I was using QuickBooks and wasn't sure of something, I would go home and reference the book for answers. If the book didn't cover the problem, I googled it.

When I was moving to Boston and left the job, I had to train my replacement, who claimed in her interview that she knew QuickBooks. I thought she knew more than I did, so I wanted to show her specific things in QuickBooks related to the amusement park's bookkeeping. She asked me generic, beginner questions about QuickBooks (like how do you sort the customer list and vendor list from A-Z or Z-A?), which revealed that she didn't actually know how to use the software at all.

I didn't want her to feel bad, so I told her I learned how to do my job by reading QuickBooks for Dummies and Bookkeeping for Dummies. No one trained me for the job. It was 100% from reading those two books alone and researching specific problems online. I recommended that she also check those books from the library. Her response: "Oh, I don't need that. I already know what I'm doing."

Two years later, that woman messaged me on Facebook complaining about my ex-boss always micromanaging her. I responded, "[Ex-boss] was actually one of my favorite bosses of all time and never micromanaged me." She was an incredibly nice woman and someone I admired in business. I don't know the truth, but my best guess is that my ex-boss started micromanaging after realizing my replacement was incompetent.

At this job, I learned how valuable it is to be an employee with a willingness to learn. I learned to be comfortable with the fact that I'm a complete beginner and that I don't know everything. Every successful person was a complete beginner who made lots of mistakes at some point. People who succeed are willing to learn instead of saying, "I don't need to learn that because I know it already."

Bookkeeper at R.S. Nazarian

This ranks as the #1 worst job I ever worked. I landed this job offer seven days after applying for jobs in Boston. I was really motivated to land a job offer quickly because I wanted a job in Boston before moving there. During the interview, the company owner told me he liked my hustle. We got along very well.

After I started working, I realized he was a micromanager. At 10:00am, he let everyone take a 15-minute break. One day, I left my desk for break at 10:01am, so I got back at 10:16am. He yelled at me for taking a 16-minute break. He also yelled at me for printing on brand-new computer paper instead of printing on the back of used computer paper. I couldn't handle the environment.

Eight weeks later, I started applying for jobs on a Tuesday morning on the train to work. By the end of the day, I had already received a request for an interview for the following Monday.

During the interview, my two future bosses asked me why I was leaving my current job. I told them I learned important lessons: to make sure my boss wasn't a micromanager and that the work culture wasn't toxic before accepting the job offer. The moment after I said this, they said, "You hate micromanagers? We hate micromanaging. You're hired."

As you can see, even at the worst jobs you ever had, there are still valuable lessons you can talk about in your job interview. Remember, it's not just about the positions you've held, it's about the narrative you weave.

Part 3

Opportunity

"Opportunity is missed by most people because it is dressed in overalls and looks like work."

—Thomas A. Edison

Chapter 42

Crafting Attention-Grabbing Resumes That Reach Hiring Managers

Resumes are merely a sales pitch to pique the hiring manager's interest in hiring you. A resume is an advertisement, no different from the advertisements you see on TV and on the Internet. The belief that a resume needs to be an accurate history of your career is false.

To land a job offer in five days, you must have the mindset of a salesperson. Salespeople tell you how this product or service is the answer to all your prayers. They highlight all the amazing benefits you will get if you buy it. They don't talk about what the product can do, which would be the equivalent of listing your career history on the resume. Instead, they talk about how the product can change your life. Your resume needs to convince the person reading it that you can improve something within the company.

By now, you should be ready to start crafting your resume. To assist you in this important task, I have created a detailed Resume Template which you can download at annieyangfinancial.com/resume-template. This template is designed to help you highlight your experiences and achievements in a manner that aligns with the principles shared in this book.

When I was first hiring for Annie Yang Financial Corporation, I received over 300 applications. First, I examined the resumes with a fine-tooth comb to make sure everyone received an equal amount of time. I hated how hiring managers looked at a resume for a few seconds and then just threw it in the discard pile. I wanted to put more care into this process.

After a while, I stopped doing that. I finally understood hiring managers. None of the resumes stood out. If I scrubbed the names from the top of the resume, I would have thought 80% of them were the same person. They all communicated that they had graduated from university, possessed experience in their fields, were quick at learning, were team players, had excellent time management, and were great communicators.

Hiring managers only spend ten seconds looking at a resume. If there are 300 and you spend one minute reading each resume, it would take five hours just to go through resumes. If you spend ten seconds each, it will take only 50 minutes to sort through 300 resumes. This is why the career advice is to limit your resume to only one page. No one has time to read beyond the first page. It's like how people read the headlines of news articles instead of reading the entire article. If they read the article, they usually only read the first couple of paragraphs to get the gist of the story.

Hiring managers don't read your resume. They don't even skim your resume. They merely glance at it and if something catches their eye, they'll do a double take and read through it more thoroughly. I know this as a fact because that's exactly what I do now when I sort through resumes.

When I looked at resumes, I thought,

"Great. You're smart and capable. But I don't care about your smarts. This company is my baby. It's my dream. How can you help me make my dreams come true? I can train any monkey to do this job because I have a training manual. It's a natural cycle that there will be downtime at work. During the downtime, are you capable of solving the big problems my company is having so my company can grow? And if you are capable, are you willing to do it? I can teach you all the skills, but I

can't teach you how to have the passion to complete the project. The best results come when you're passionate about what you're doing. If you lack passion, I'll assign you the project and you'll drag your feet. You'll frustrate me beyond belief."

I'm sure I'm not the only hiring manager who feels this way.

Many people think the resume is a deal breaker, but it's not, because the fact is, I spend only 10 seconds looking at someone's resume. And even then, that doesn't become the major deal breaker for me. A deal breaker for me is how they answer my screening question. Other employers hire differently, so the deal breaker for them might not be the screening question—it could be something else.

Tailoring Your Resume Based on a Master Resume

An easy way to create a tailored resume is to create a master resume first that lists all your jobs and accomplishments. The master resume can be as long as you want. When you're applying to jobs within a specific industry or for a specific job title, you can quickly copy and paste the relevant information from the master resume to create a customized version. Remember, keep the tailored resume to one page maximum.

Full Contact Information

Put your full contact information at the top of your resume: your full name, phone number, address, and email address with your custom domain name. As discussed in Chapter 21: Registering a Custom Domain Email Address for Free, use an email address with your custom domain name because it leads people to check out your website.

It's important to put your full contact information. Do not assume that the hiring manager or recruiter can find your contact information through the job board website. When I was hiring for my company through Hubstaff Talent, I wanted to reach out to every single job applicant on the status of their application, even when it was a rejection. I messaged 300 people one by one. The problem was that when I messaged 50 people, Hubstaff Talent flagged me as a spammer. They would block my account from sending messages for 24 hours. The next day I would message 50 more people. Getting my account temporarily blocked was a problem because there was no way for me to contact the applicants that I wanted to interview.

There was one particular candidate who I had initially messaged asking her to answer a screening question. I liked her answers and wanted to move forward, but when I tried to message her again through the site, it kept giving an error about her profile not being confirmed. Her full contact information was also missing from her resume. By pure luck, she had written her answers in a shared Google Doc, so I was able to find her Gmail address. Had she supplied her screening answers directly within the Hubstaff messaging system, I would not have been able to contact her.

Accomplishments, Not Job Duties

All the resumes I read from accountants were very similar. On their resumes, they had their job duties listed, but not their accomplishments. Accountants have similar responsibilities and tasks regardless of which company they work for. While I was reading the resumes, I wondered what made this candidate better than another candidate if they both did the same thing, but at a different company?

The key to differentiating yourself is to only write about your accomplishments. Hiring managers and recruiters can safely assume what your job duties were based on the job title you held. An Accounts Receivable clerk will always be someone who creates invoices, collects money from clients, and records the payment in the system. An Accounts Payable clerk will always enter bills in the accounting system and pay them. A bookkeeper will always reconcile bank and credit card accounts and do month end adjustments. There is no point in parroting this again and again in different words, yet people in accounting keep doing this on their resume.

What did you accomplish at the job? What did you improve? What projects did you work on outside of your essential job duties? What problems did you solve at work? For example, something I wrote on my resume that caught the eye of my future boss was, "Triple checked the paperwork from prior years and calculated that $50,000.00 held in escrow actually belonged to the company."

Sounds impressive? You bet it does. That's the line that landed me an interview.

At the interview, my future boss asked me for more details about the story behind that line.

The company I worked for kept money in its escrow account, but the prior bookkeepers weren't too attentive to detail. I wanted to check their work, so I went through all the paperwork one by one in my spare time. Since the company's inception, the bookkeepers would transfer less than they were supposed to, or they would forget to transfer it for one deal here and there (one deal averaged $3,000.00). So they only had to mess up around 16 times for it to add up to $50,000.00. For a five-year-old company, that was around three screw ups a year—no one would have noticed that. I transferred the $50,000.00 to the company's operating account, so it was almost like finding free money to spend. To my future boss, this story showed him I was someone who took initiative and cared about doing something outside of my normal job responsibilities.

The best way for a future employer to judge what they can expect from you at work is by looking at what you already did in the past. To my future boss's delight, within a month, I examined the company's health insurance policy and found that we were paying a health insurance premium for an employee who had resigned three months ago. I called the health insurance company and got a $6,000.00 refund. Another employee wouldn't have questioned the bill like I did—the bill was on autopay, so they most likely would have just filed the bill away.

These two examples from my life were easy for me to think of. If you've worked at a company for at least one year, there is no doubt you've been assigned projects to work on during slow times. Write them on your resume.

Bullet Points

You should use bullet points in your resume to list your accomplishments. Don't write paragraphs. Limit each bullet point to one line only.

Active Voice

For each bullet point, describe what you did and what you accomplished using a verb as the first word. For example, write "Created a new system for organizing receipts," instead of "I created a new system for organizing receipts."

Your verbs must be past tense for previous jobs and present tense for the job you're currently employed in.

Remember to use active voice instead of passive voice. An example of passive voice is, "A new system for organizing receipts was created by me." The active voice version would be, "Created a new system for organizing receipts." Explaining English is beyond the scope of this book. If you're unfamiliar with how to change your sentences from passive voice to active voice, you can read the article, "Changing Passive to Active Voice" by Purdue University.

Additionally, to make your achievements stand out, I highly recommend using powerful verbs. These verbs can help communicate your achievements more effectively and assertively. I have compiled a list of 400 Power Verbs for Effective Resumes that you can use as a handy reference while writing your resume. You can download it at annieyangfinancial.com/resume-verbs.

Consistent Formatting

The job title, company name, and years worked all need to be in a consistent format. For example, you should not format the job title for one of your jobs in italic, and then format another job title in bold with underline.

White Space

Pay attention to the formatting of your resume. Design matters just as much as content. People make the font smaller, reduce the line spacing, and make the margins narrower to make everything fit when they are limited to one page. The result is a cluttered and cramped resume. It's hard to read because the eyes don't know where to look first.

The resume needs to have a balanced amount of white space so people can easily see the different sections of your resume when it's held at arm's length. If you're not sure, ask your friends to look over your resume and give you honest feedback about the white space.

Stupid Typos

At one of my former jobs, I knew it was my coworker who had looked at my resume and passed it on to the company owners to review. I asked her why my resume made it through her filters. After all, plenty of people applied for the job, but I was the only one who got an interview.

She told me it was because all the other resumes had stupid little mistakes. She showed me resumes from the other applicants. One of them spelled "bookkeeper" as "bookeeper." Many of them were inconsistent in their resume formatting (bold, italics, underline). She cared about these kinds of things because bookkeeping is a detail-oriented job. The resumes clearly showed the candidates did not pay attention to detail.

When hiring for my company, one particular applicant typed his pronoun, "I" in lowercase. If it were only once, I would have glossed over it. However, his screening answer was littered with lowercase "I"s all over. I immediately discarded his application because I can't have someone representing my company to clients and vendors by typing like that. If people saw those kinds of typos in any email communication, they would have thought my company was being run by middle school students. I can train people on how to do the job, but it's not my responsibility to train people on how to write correctly. I give slack to international applicants whose first language isn't English, but only in terms of grammar. Spelling mistakes don't receive any grace from me because candidates can easily fix them with spellcheck.

Resume Writers

If you really need help with writing a resume, your best bet is to pay a resume writer to do it for you. Writing isn't a strength for everybody, and you need to take advantage of every resource you can to land a job in five days. There is no shame in paying for professional help when you're weak at something.

Final Look-Through

Don't assume everyone will understand the content of your resume. If you use too many technical words and jargon to sound smart, it could actually backfire. Especially in accounting, because many small business owners looking to hire an accountant don't have specialized accounting knowledge—that's the entire point of why they are hiring an accountant. If you use fancy words and acronyms, they won't understand what you're saying, and they aren't going to take the time to figure out what you mean.

The same thing happens when recruiters are looking at the resume first before passing it to the hiring manager. The recruiter aids the hiring process but does not have the same level of understanding that the hiring manager does regarding what it's like to do the job and what skills are really needed. You need to dumb down your resume for people lacking the specialized, technical knowledge.

To solve this problem, ask several friends outside of your industry to read your resume. Ask them what they think you accomplished in your job. If they can't answer the question, you have a problem. Ask them what was unclear. Revise your resume and ask them to read it again. Keep revising until it all makes sense.

Chapter 43

Boosting Your Interview Chances by Applying to 50 Jobs Daily

If you want to land a job offer in five days, don't expect it to happen if you only apply for five jobs.

It's like hearing your single girlfriend bemoan being in the dating scene for the last five years. You ask her how many dates she's went on in the last 12 months. She tells you, "So many!" Most people listening will stop and accept her complaints at face value. They might even show empathy by sharing how difficult their experiences were.

My single girlfriend complained about how she went on so many dates with people and was still single. Instead of accepting her story, I pressed her for details. "How many dates did you go on in the last 12 months?"

"Six dates," she said. That's a rate of one date every two months.

"Why only six?" I asked.

"It was because there was always one little thing that I didn't like about every single dating profile I looked at," she answered.

She never even contacted them. When I heard this, it was painstakingly obvious why she made zero progress. She judged people before they even got a chance to speak to her. She didn't go out with enough men to find the right one!

If I were in her shoes, I would go on three dates a week! I'm serious! I would ask everyone I spoke to if they knew a guy that was single and looking. That is precisely what I did when I decided I wanted to find a husband. I met my husband one month after I set a goal to find one.

I didn't know I would end up meeting him through Craigslist. I was actually getting ready to go on date match websites like Christian Mingle. I would have followed a game plan: spend Monday, Tuesday, Wednesday, and Thursday chatting with guys on various dating apps. I wouldn't have cared what their profiles looked like. They could have even been blank! What mattered was whether the spark was there. You can never tell if the spark exists until you start talking to each other. I would have messaged all the guys on the site and focused on following up with the ones who messaged back.

Then I would have scheduled one date for Friday, one for Saturday, and one for Sunday. Three dates a week means 156 dates a year. There is no way the right man doesn't exist in that pool of 156. He's definitely somewhere in there. If he's not in there, you need to look in the mirror because I bet the problem is your standards are so high that no one could ever meet them.

Next time you hear someone complaining about their job search, press them about their approach and job-hunting philosophy. Everyone has one. They might have a job-hunting philosophy similar to my single girlfriend's dating philosophy. They only want to work for a select 20 companies. They predetermine that only those 20 companies are the best fit for their career through research, even though they've never interacted with anyone from that company. They craft the perfect resume and job application. Then, they wait and wait and wait. Crickets. When they don't hear back from any of the 20 companies, they're in tough luck.

What are they going to do? Keep stalking the company until another job position opens so they can apply again? Some people actually do that. The truth is, they're just not that into you.

I approach job hunting the same way I approach dating: systematically. Getting a job is a two-way street. You have to be interested in that company, but that company also has to be interested in you. "You catch more fish with a net than with a fishing rod." Don't bother researching any of the companies. Just apply. If you apply to 50 companies every day for one week, after one week, you'll have applied for 350 jobs. I've had a lot of luck applying for jobs on Indeed and ZipRecruiter, but job boards really depend on your industry.

Don't be afraid to apply for job listings that are over 30 days old. The listings are stale and many people have applied already, but that doesn't mean they've already hired. It's possible none of the applicants were qualified. If the listing is still up, it's free game. It never hurts to apply. It only hurts to not apply.

Keeping track of your job applications is another crucial aspect of a successful job search. You don't want to seem like a spammer by accidentally applying for the same position twice. It's also beneficial to have a record of job listings when preparing for an interview. Instead of wrestling with copying and pasting URLs into an excel sheet, you can streamline this process using the Job Application Tracker I've created. This tool is designed to help you stay organized and can be downloaded at annieyangfinancial.com/track-jobs.

After applying for a job, it's a good idea to follow up. However, this can be a daunting task if you're unsure what to say or how to say it. To make this process easier for you, I've created a set of job application follow-up email templates. Download these templates at annieyangfinancial.com/job-email. They are designed to help you professionally and effectively communicate with potential employers.

When you don't hear back from a company, it's nothing personal. Don't take it personally, especially at this stage. For all you know, the reason you didn't hear back was because the person in charge of looking through the resumes went on vacation. There is nothing wrong with you. Don't make this about you. It may be personal if I committed time to an interview and got rejected. Even then, I've learned that the best reaction to getting rejected is to look at it as a blessing in disguise.

It helps to create your own definition of success. I define success as getting one job offer. I don't need ten job offers. When you look at it this way, you won't feel as crummy when you don't hear back from all the companies you applied to.

If you hear back from 2% of the 350 companies, you'll get seven interviews. When you land an interview, it means that the company is interested in you. This is the stage where you thoroughly research every single company offering you an interview.

Chapter 44

Researching Companies to Tailor Your Interview Strategy

The dreaded job interviews. Even the most experienced and qualified professionals hate job interviews. It's a contest. You compete with all the other applicants to show that you are better. This mindset leads job candidates to talk about how brilliant they are, how they graduated from a top school, and how they've worked for well-known companies.

How can you learn to enjoy the process and excel at it?

Eighty percent of giving a great interview begins with doing the homework before the interview: researching the company. There are many books and articles stressing the importance of researching the company. They say it's so important because you need to display interest, curiosity, and enthusiasm for the company. But that's the wrong reason. Plus, none of those books ever go into the step-by-step process on how to do research.

The entire goal of research is to get inside the interviewer's head. Once you uncover the problem that drives everyone crazy in the company, you show that you're the right person for the job, since you have the solutions.

The interview conversation should not be about you. The interview itself is proof that you qualify. Focus the conversation on the company and how you fit into the overall picture.

To help you prepare for your interview and ensure you don't miss any critical research, I've created an Interview Preparation

Checklist. Visit annieyangfinancial.com/interview-checklist to download this helpful resource.

Once you've downloaded the checklist, let's dive into the different areas you should focus your research:

Research the Official Website

Start by exploring all the pages on their official website for a basic overview of how the company provides value to its customers. If the website has poor navigation functionality or isn't well organized, you can generate a sitemap and read all the pages with MySiteMapGenerator.com.

Research Social Media Pages

Check out everything the company has posted in the last year on Facebook, Instagram, Twitter, LinkedIn, YouTube, TikTok, and all the other popular social media platforms. Take notes on what they are currently doing and add your own notes on how they could do it even better. For example, at a company I used to work, we would run a "Spot A Red Tree" photo contest where everyone in the community could snap a picture of a red tree during fall foliage and post it with the hashtag #SpotARedTree on Facebook. The contest ran for a month, and we announced winners every week and awarded various prized tickets to a game or a movie. It was our way of building relationships with people in the community who might later want to put their house up for sale through us.

Before I left the company, the partners asked me to join the interview for my potential replacement. The "Spot A Red Tree" contest had just ended. One of the company partners asked her what she thought of our social media. She said, "I looked at your social media and I thought you guys were doing a great job at it." I asked her precisely what she liked about our social media. Was it the branding? Was it a specific post? She couldn't answer the question. She got the job anyway because there were no outstanding candidates willing to work for the salary published on the job listing, but that's winning by default—not winning because you were outstanding.

She did not impress me. She could have mentioned the "Spot A Red Tree" contest and a bunch of other community initiatives we posted. Had she been extra prepared, she could have also used the opportunity to show us some posts that other companies (any company—not necessarily a competitor) were doing on social media that she really liked and thought we could implement at our company. That would have conveyed she was the kind of person who could generate ideas to help the company grow.

When you do your research, you'll find at some companies, the social media marketing is nonexistent. At other companies, they created their social media pages, but they haven't updated anything in the last three years.

You can still turn this into a strength in your interview. Use it as an opportunity to ask about their current marketing strategy and why you can't find very much information about the company through social media. Tell the interviewer you want to be part of a company that has a vision and focus for the future. You don't want to work for a company that simply skates by, content with making the same amount of money they made last year. You want a company that makes more money year after year so you can make more money too. Making more money with each passing year doesn't happen by accident. It requires detailed planning.

If the interviewer says they don't currently have a proper marketing strategy, offer some of your own ideas that might help. If they show enthusiasm for your ideas, that's a sign you'll be welcomed after you're hired. If you get a low-energy reaction, it means the people working there hate change and would rather keep doing things the way they are.

Research Reviews From Employees

Glassdoor is a website to get insight into the interview questions and salaries offered for various jobs. You don't need that. If you practiced Table Topics exercises discussed in Chapter 28:

Mastering Public Speaking to Answer Tough Interview Questions, you should be able to handle any questions with ease.

On Glassdoor, focus on the reviews written by employees. What do they love and hate about the company? Take notes on the trends you find.

When you're a star candidate at an interview, the interviewer is trying his best to sell you the dream. The interviewer is trying to convince you to accept the offer from that company. Play devil's advocate. Poke holes in the sales pitch with contradictory information you found online, whether it's the micromanagement, the inflexible hours, or toxic culture. Ask why there is a discrepancy between how the interviewers paint the company vs. what employees actually think.

Tell the interviewer you have many job options, and you want to work for a company that's the best fit for you, so you need to do careful vetting. Describe the various negative opinions that employees have posted about working there. Ask the interviewer whether he agrees with those opinions. If he agrees, ask him what the company is doing to solve the problem. If he disagrees and says the reviews were written by disgruntled employees who were fired for not performing at a certain standard, ask him for real examples and evidence to back up his statement.

As for you saying, "I have many job options," that's the truth for everyone. Even if you haven't gotten a job offer from any company yet, you always have choices in life. No one can force you to do anything. You always have a choice in how you want to earn money.

Research Reviews From Customers

Check the reviews from customers on Google, Yelp, Better Business Bureau, Trust Pilot, Consumer Affairs, and all the other specialized review sites in the industry.

If you notice that most of the customer reviews are great, you can mention that you want to work for a company that has created such an excellent reputation. If the customer reviews are poor, flip it around and tell the interviewer you're rather hesitant because according to your research, many customers are unhappy with the products or services, but you're open-minded so you're willing to hear the company's side of the story. It's important to work at a company with a great reputation because it affects your personal reputation by association. If a company has a poor reputation and you list it on your resume in the future, your job application might end up in the trash.

Research the Company Owner

At large corporations, it's easy to find the CEO and read about his life. But at small companies, you might have to dig around because he prefers to keep that information private. All corporations and limited liability companies need to be registered with the Secretary of State. This is public information. Search for the company's name in your state's corporate database. You should be able to find the names of all the officers. You can Google their names and look at their personal social media to see what their interests are. Maybe you have common ground outside of work and can use the mutual interests as a conversation starter if you end up meeting them.

Research the Team

Some companies showcase their team on the About page of their website. If they don't have a page about the team, check LinkedIn to find out who works there. The information might be outdated, but it's a good start. Check LinkedIn and other social media profiles of the people you might end up working with. This way, when you're in the interview, you can sound like you already work there and ask about how you'll be working with those specific individuals.

Check to see if you have any mutual friends with anyone on the team. If you live in a small town, chances are you do. Privately ask the mutual friends what they know.

Research the Industry

What is the current state of the industry? Research the news (national, local, and industry specific) to uncover how recent events could affect the company. If you're getting interviewed by a big company, research the news to check if the company itself was mentioned. Reading about the industry will help you uncover any problems the company might experience so you can think of solutions to bring to the interview.

Create a List of Questions

After you finish your research and take notes, create a list of questions to ask the interviewer that will help you determine whether YOU want to even work there. Many people treat a job interview like it's some sort of police interrogation. Or just like with dating, they pray and hope the other person likes them back.

Interviews are a two-way street! Stop focusing on the great new salary. Pay attention to the things that might affect your quality of life. This is your chance to figure out if the company has a high turnover problem because of a toxic work culture, whether you'll be working under a micromanager, or if there's an unspoken rule that everyone should work overtime in the office until 10pm, every day. Maybe the company is having cash flow problems, so when the financials take a turn for the worse, they will lay off immediately.

The best questions are specific to the research you did and to what you discussed in the interview.

However, here are some generic questions to inspire you to get started:

Questions About Company Strategy

- What is the company's business strategy and how does this position fit into the grand scheme of things?
- Where do you personally think the company is headed in the next five years?

Questions About Culture

- How would you describe the culture here?
- If this is a remote position, how do employees get integrated into the company culture?
- What do new employees typically find surprising after they start?
- Is there something I should read before starting this job?
- What's your favorite office tradition?
- What do you and the team usually do for lunch?
- Do you ever have events with other departments or teams?
- What is different about working here than anywhere else you've worked?

Questions About the Interviewer

- How long have you been at this company?
- How long have you been working as a manager here?
- What is your favorite part about working here?
- How has the company changed since you started working here?
- What do you enjoy about your job?
- What did you wish you knew before you joined the company?

Questions About Job Responsibilities

- What are the biggest challenges I would face in this position?
- What skills are currently missing from the existing team members?
- What does a typical day for me in this role look like?
- Earlier in the interview, you mentioned I would be responsible for a project that wasn't stated in the job description. Could you tell me more about this project?
- What are your expectations for me in this role?

- What is the most important thing I should accomplish in the first 90 days?
- What is the performance review process here like? How often do you do a performance review?
- What are the most immediate projects I would take on?
- How long would it be before I interact with clients/vendors?
- Would my primary responsibilities change after six months? After one year?
- Who will I be working with most closely?
- What other departments would I interact with?
- Who are my direct reports? What are their strengths and biggest challenges?

Questions About Career Development

- What learning and development opportunities will I have in this role?
- What kind of professional development and training does this company provide?
- Can you give me some examples of career paths people went on after starting at this same position?
- What are common career paths for people in this department?
- How are promotions typically handled?
- Where have successful employees moved onto?

Questions About the Previous Employee

- Why is the position open? Is this a brand-new position or am I replacing somebody?
- Why did the previous employee leave?
- What did the previous employee do incredibly well that you would like to see the replacement continue?

Chapter 45

Mastering Fearless Salary Negotiation for the Best Offer

Salary offers are not pulled out of thin air. Companies research market rates for job titles in specific geographic areas and establish a pay range. No set salary number exists, as it depends on the individuals and how much value the company perceives they will bring. Ideal candidates receive high-end pay, while those needing more training and experience get paid at the lower end. This doesn't apply to places like McDonald's, where everyone gets paid equally regardless of experience.

The pay range explains why a manager could be paid less than an individual contributor. A manager might be paid in the low-end range, with potential for future increases, while an individual contributor could be maxed out at the high-end range, with no pay raise unless they get a new job title with a different pay range.

You don't have insider information on the company's finances to negotiate salary effectively. However, you can conduct the same research the company did to establish a pay range, so when you request more money, your reasoning is based on facts rather than a general claim that you deserve more money "just because."

To help you with this, you can download the Salary Research Worksheet at annieyangfinancial.com/salary-research. This tool will guide you in organizing the data you collect in your salary research.

Researching can help you determine whether you've been low-balled or not. To research salaries, simply Google the job title you applied for and "salary." Open all the search results in new tabs and copy and paste the salary from each website into an Excel sheet. If there's another job title with similar job duties, research that too. This entire exercise should take no more than one hour.

I highly recommend two books that immensely helped my negotiations. Read them well in advance of your job interview, just in case the interviewer asks you, "What's your desired salary?" (trick question). The correct answer is, "I want to be paid according to the value my skills and experience bring to your organization." Let the company propose the first number. It's possible the initial number is higher than what you had in mind. If you answer first and it's lower than what they planned to offer, they'll give you exactly what you answered.

The first book is *Fearless Salary Negotiation: A Step-By-Step Guide To Getting Paid What You're Worth* by Josh Doody. This book is expensive, and I couldn't find it at my local library, but I took the plunge because $50.00 isn't much if it helps me negotiate a few thousand dollars more. Doody's book explains salary negotiation better than I could ever attempt.

The second book is *Never Split the Difference: Negotiating as if Your Life Depended on It* by Chris Voss. Voss explains how to negotiate in high-pressure situations. Negotiating a salary is stressful because it's not something you do daily. If you negotiated salaries every day, it would feel easy. But the fact is, most people do this kind of negotiation once every 2-3 years, while employers negotiate every time they hire someone new. You don't have enough practice to do this well. The most important concept in Voss's book is the idea of odd numbers. He also explains this concept within the context of salary negotiation. Follow his method.

For help structuring your email response during the salary negotiation process, you can download the Salary Negotiation Email Template at <u>annieyangfinancial.com/salary-email</u>.

After mastering salary negotiation, it's essential to think about what benefits matter most to you. A job is more than just a means to earn a living—it influences your lifestyle and overall happiness. Be realistic about your desires. For example, I would personally negotiate work arrangements and education benefits, as those are my priorities.

Here are various aspects you can negotiate after finalizing your salary to help you envision the bigger picture of your life and finances.

Work Arrangement

- Job Title
- Fully Remote or Hybrid Work
- Flexible Schedule
- Office Space

Starting the New Job

- Start Date
- Signing Bonus
- Relocation Expenses

Time Off

- Vacation Time
- Personal Leave
- Sick Leave
- Parental Leave
- Bereavement Leave

Commuting

- Company Car
- Transportation Reimbursement
- Paid Parking

Insurance

- Health Insurance
- Dental Insurance
- Vision Insurance
- Disability Insurance
- Life Insurance Plans

Financial

- Retirement Plans + 401(k) Matching
- Severance Package
- Stock Options or Other Long-Term Incentives
- Equity

Education

- Student Loan Repayment
- Mentoring Opportunities
- Tuition, Training, and Continuing Education
- Professional Development Opportunities

Miscellaneous

- Retainable Airline Miles
- Childcare Reimbursement
- Discounts on Company Products
- Earlier Performance Review
- Health and Wellness Benefits
- Professional Associations or Subscription Reimbursement
- Work Phone or Laptop

To help you with negotiating benefits, I have also created a Benefits Negotiation Email Template. Download it at annieyang-financial.com/benefits-email.

Chapter 46

Harnessing Personal Power to Boost Interview Performance

Dress to Impress

Your first impression speaks volumes. As much as some people like to downplay the significance of appearance, you need to put work into it. I'm not saying you need to look like a supermodel, but you should put your best foot forward by dressing to impress.

I'm surprised by how some people show up for an interview. One woman was wearing a slouchy knit sweater to an accounting job interview. Accounting is a profession that demands order and precision, and the clothes should communicate your attention to detail.

The same advice applies here as in Chapter 16: Creating a Lasting First Impression with a Professional Headshot and Chapter 25: Presenting Your Best Self in Every Situation.

We must pay attention to the details that we might have overlooked during the headshot photoshoot this time since it is in-person.

First, trim your nails. If you get a manicure, keep it simple. Anything too flashy would be too distracting.

Second, if you ate breakfast or lunch, check if there's any food stuck in your teeth. Check your breath. Does it stink? Carry a travel-sized bottle of mouthwash and use it right before your interview.

Third, go light on perfume. Some people are sensitive to fragrances and the interviewer could feel too nauseous to pay attention to what you're saying.

Fourth, don't wear statement jewelry. Don't wear jewelry that make a lot of noise, like bangle bracelets. You want the interviewer's attention to be on the conversation and not on your jewelry.

The point is to appear pleasant. Ask yourself, "If I were a pleasant person, what would I do differently?" Think about it.

Bring Your Resume

Don't assume they already have your resume printed. People are busy. Some are juggling multiple projects and meetings. Your resume might be in the email inbox of someone who is out of the office that day. The office printer broke that day.

Your interviewer has your resume somewhere in her email inbox, but have you seen people's email inboxes nowadays? Sometimes when people are playing on their phone, I peer over their shoulder, and I see they have 4,993 unread emails according to the red badge icon displayed on the email app. The first time I saw that, I was so shocked because I read every single email I receive and make sure none of my work falls through the cracks. But over the years, I realized it's incredibly common for people to have 3,000+ unread work emails. People are extremely unorganized at work. This explains why so many people never respond to you. Your email seems to get sucked into a black hole. They don't even read their emails to begin with. Don't let other people's disorganized chaos ruin your chance at getting a great job interview.

Print several copies of your resume and bring them with you on the day of your interview. You never know how many people at the company will walk into the room to say hi or ask you a few quick questions. If they want a copy of your resume, the interviewer might feel inconvenienced by having to walk to the copy machine and make copies.

Imagine the interviewer at the copy machine trying to make copies of your resume, and the paper gets jammed, or the ink cartridge needs to be replaced. It's like everything that could go wrong is going wrong. This would be a great comedy skit, but it's your worst nightmare in real life.

If you want to go the extra mile, print your resume with your personal branding colors. If you don't have a color printer, it's only around $0.65 per printed page at FedEx or Staples. Printing 5 copies would cost $3.25. Chump change. Spend a little money for a lot of style.

Put Your Documents Into a Folder

Buy a nice-looking folder to keep all your documents. It will make you look more professional and organized. It's only $2.00. There is no excuse not to do this.

This is what you need to put into your nice-looking folder:

- Several copies of your resume
- A printed copy of the job listing so you can point out your questions during the interview
- The notes from the research you did in Chapter 44: Researching Companies to Tailor Your Interview Strategy
- The specific questions based on your research in Chapter 44: Researching Companies to Tailor Your Interview Strategy
- Blank paper in case you need to take notes on something the interviewer says

Have all of this ready well before the day of the interview. Put the folder into your bag so you won't forget it. Don't forget to pack a pen in your bag.

Being prepared this way will give you peace of mind and help you relax on the big day.

And here, I would like to point out a resource that can help streamline this process, an Interview Preparation Checklist, which you can find and download at <u>annieyangfinancial.com/interview-checklist</u>. It can assist in keeping your research, questions, and other vital aspects of interview preparation neatly organized and at your fingertips.

Arriving Early Is Arriving on Time

Arrive for the interview fifteen minutes early. If you arrive too early, you'll be inconveniencing people in the middle of doing something. If you arrive only five minutes before, you won't be able to start the interview on time. Fifteen minutes will give you enough time to enter a lobby at a high-rise office building and deal with security. It could give you time to wait for the elevator. Maybe you can get lost inside the building—that's happened to me before.

Furthermore, I've discovered that many interviewers are un-prepared when walking into an interview. Many companies don't have a systematic approach to the hiring process, where they ask everyone the same questions so that every candidate gets a fair shot. They wrongly believe that hiring a star employee is one of those "I know it when I see it" kind of things, so they never create an official interviewing process for identifying who should get the job and who shouldn't.

Because they don't have good questions prepared, they end up asking half-baked questions based on what stood out to them when they were quickly skimming your resume. Therefore, if you arrive early, you'll at least give the interviewer time to glance over your resume and come up with conversation starters and half-baked questions while also having an inner panic attack that the interview is about to start.

How to Make Sure You Show Up Exactly Fifteen Minutes Early

Do a test run a few days before the interview. Drive or take public transit to the actual site. This way you know exactly which exit on the highway to take and in which lane to drive so you don't miss it. Also, learn exactly where to wait for your bus or train transfer. Look around the building and find the proper entrance to know exactly which door to walk through on the day of the interview.

On the day of the interview, arrive one hour early and hang out at a café or public library while you wait. Look on Google Maps to see precisely how long it will take to walk to the entrance of the office building and time your walk so that you will get there exactly fifteen minutes early.

When I worked in the office, I would always walk through the door between 8:58am and 9:00am. My boss thought I had somehow mastered the public transit system. One day, there was a snowstorm, and I still walked in at my usual time. He was shocked. He couldn't grasp how I kept timing the bus so perfectly. I couldn't help but laugh. Every morning, I arrived one hour early to a nearby café and bought a $2.00 tea and worked on my personal projects. At 8:50 am, I would walk to the office. That was my secret to arriving at the same time every single morning, no matter what. You'll hardly ever find me blaming traffic or public transit delays for why I'm late. When I actually use an external circumstance as the reason, people are always very forgiving. They know I am telling the truth because I'm always punctual.

Chapter 47

Projecting Confidence to Increase Interview Success Rates

If you follow every single piece of advice already discussed in this book, you've already completed eighty percent of the legwork for a successful interview before the interview has even started. To help you keep track of all these pieces of advice and ensure you're well-prepared, I've prepared an Interview Prep Checklist. Download it at annieyangfinancial.com/interview-checklist.

I discussed how to answer interview questions with confidence in Chapter 28: Mastering Public Speaking to Answer Tough Interview Questions. If you don't remember, go back and re-read that section.

Energy is an intangible quality. The remaining 20% factor that will land you the job offer is your energy. No one can see it with their eyes, but they can feel it. Energy is a real thing.

Develop the ability to command your energy at will. Think of the last time someone wanted something from you. The pushier they became, the more you wanted to scream "NO!" just to show them who is really in control. But if the person told you what they wanted without expecting anything specific from you, you would probably be more inclined to volunteer and offer to help them get what they want. At least, you would point them in the right direction because you want to be a good person. This is the difference in the energy. You show up differently in the world when you can control your energy. You change the conversations you have with people when they perceive you differently.

Some job candidates have energy that reeks of desperation. They don't get the job. Desperation is never good. It leaves a poor impression and makes people trust you less. When you're desperate for a job or money, how far will you be willing to go to get the money? Would you go as far as lying on your resume? Maybe even stealing money after getting hired?

Unfortunately, you can't mask desperation. You can't fake energy. It has to be authentic. The only solution is to truly feel, deep within your soul, an energy that says you don't need the job—you want the job for good reasons, and getting paid good money to do it is simply a bonus. Perhaps the job aligns with your life purpose. Maybe you strongly believe this job is the best way you can serve people with your gifts and talents. When you come from a place of desire, people are more inspired and attuned to giving you what you want.

How do you go from thinking, "I need the job because I need to make money to pay my bills," to, "I want the job because it's a great opportunity, but if I don't get the job, I'm still okay"?

Change Your Current Frame of Reference

The first step is to change your current frame of reference. Your current frame of reference is what you currently believe about your circumstances. Your circumstances do not determine how your life turns out. The truth is, what you think and how you feel about your circumstances determine the actions you end up taking. Your actions determine your future. It's why two people who started with the same or similar circumstances can have completely different results. We each have agency to choose how to react to life.

Your mind is powerful. Your energy flows according to whatever you focus on.

I recently came across a self-coaching system for working on your thoughts by Brooke Castillo from the Life Coach School Podcast. I've been using her system with a lot of success. This is the method:

First, examine your thoughts about looking for a new job. Dump all your thoughts quickly onto a sheet of paper. What comes up for you when you think about your current circumstance?

Here are some examples of what might come up for you.

- My current job pays the bills, but I hate my work.
- My boss won't stop micromanaging me.
- My coworkers make me feel inadequate and stupid.
- I'm really depending on landing this job offer so that I can pay my bills and not end up homeless.
- It's not possible to make money doing what you love.
- It's totally normal to spend 40 hours a week doing work you don't care about and then spend your life outside of work on activities that excite you.
- I suck at job interviews.
- I just want to get this whole thing over with already.
- I don't think I can ever make $100,000.00 a year.
- I'm not capable of getting a job that's better than what I have now.
- I don't have the education or qualifications to land that job.
- Who am I to think I can land a job offer in five days?
- No one is ever going to hire me.
- The economy is bad right now.

Second, pick one thought to work on.

Let's use "I suck at job interviews" as an example.

What is the circumstance that is creating this thought? The circumstance needs to be objective and neutral. If you word the circumstance in a way that triggers you emotionally, that's a sign that you haven't neutralized it enough.

The circumstance for "I suck at job interviews," could be "My job interview is four days from now."

Third, how does the thought, "I suck at job interviews," make you feel?

Do you feel dread? Incapable? Anxious? Insecure? Helpless? Paralyzed? Scared? Stressed? Worried?

Your answer should be one word only.

In case you have trouble finding the right word, you can download the Emotional Mastery Guide: Transforming Your Thought Process to Achieve Results, which includes a list of 450 emotions. The guide is available at annieyangfinancial.com/emotions.

We will work with the feeling, anxious.

Fourth, what actions do you take as a result of feeling anxious? Maybe you go down a rabbit hole reading stories on the internet about the worst job interview experiences. Maybe you replay in your head repeatedly all the times you messed up in job interviews in the past. Maybe you're so anxious about the upcoming interview, you're not 100% focused on doing the research and homework that was assigned in Chapter 44: Researching Companies to Tailor Your Interview Strategy. Perhaps you do the opposite and you're overzealous in your research to get rid of the anxiety and end up overthinking every unimportant detail. Maybe your anxiety gives you insomnia for four nights in a row, so you don't feel well rested.

Fifth, what's the result? You do poorly in your job interview. It's a self-fulfilling prophecy. People sabotage themselves like this all the time.

What if, working with the same circumstance, we had a completely different thought?

- Circumstance: My job interview is four days from now.
- Thought: I can't wait to do this interview! It's the first step toward my new future.
- Feeling: Excited.
- Action: I imagine all the great people I'll potentially work with in the future. I do my research and 100% of the rec-

ommended prep work, like driving to the office the day before, so I know the route. I go to sleep on time every night. I try on different outfits and launder and iron the one I will wear for the interview.

- Result: I walk into the interview, confident and ready to go.

Let's try another one:
- Circumstance: I'm unemployed.
- Thought: I'm really depending on landing this job offer so that I can pay my bills and not end up homeless.
- Feeling: Fearful.
- Action: This is the only job interview I have lined up and I really need this one to work out for me, so I give answers I think the interviewer wants to hear. I stutter in the interview because the fear is so strong that the words don't come out naturally.
- Result: I'm not an impressive candidate.

We can work with the same circumstance and change the thought:
- Circumstance: I'm unemployed.
- Thought: This is a great opportunity for me to make a career change because I wouldn't have the courage to pivot if I still had a job.
- Feeling: Grateful.
- Action: I create a plan that entails what I will do if I run out of money, whether that's moving in with my parents or friends for discounted rent, living in my car temporarily, finding out where the food shelters are, and calling utility companies to ask to be put on a payment plan. I reflect on what my next step should be. I read books and articles on how to change careers successfully and talk about my experiences and skills in an unrelated field in a way that conveys strength.

- Result: I land a job that's a great entry point for a new career.

Let's create a model for the guidance counselor who told me I would be a failure:
- Circumstance: My guidance counselor said I was destined to be a failure if I didn't go straight to college.
- Thought: She's an adult, so she must be right.
- Feeling: Resigned.
- Action: I don't look for mentors. I don't reach out to explore what options are available for someone like me. I only apply to minimum wage jobs because that's all I'm capable of. I believe the only way to make more money is to work more hours, so I make up for the lack of better pay by working 2-3 jobs at all times. I live paycheck to paycheck because what's the point? I might as well enjoy all my money now because I won't have a retirement fund anyway. I get into a relationship with a man who doesn't believe in me and ends up taking advantage of my insecurities. He takes my money because he says he's better at managing money than me.
- Result: I don't have a successful career.

But my life did not turn out that way. I responded to her words with a different thought:
- Circumstance: My guidance counselor said I was destined to be a failure if I didn't go straight to college.
- Thought: I will prove you wrong and make you take your words back.
- Feeling: Determined.
- Action: I go to the library every week and read books on subjects that interest me. I spend a lot of time reflecting on what I really want out of life. I save 25-50% of my income at every job. I learn strategies on how to live frugally so my money can go further even though I don't make a

lot of money. I look for free or extremely affordable resources that can help me develop the skills to progress in my career. I watch YouTube videos and read stories of successful people doing what I want to do. I create action plans for every goal that I set and work it into my calendar to make sure I follow through with my plans.

- Result: I graduate with my bachelor's degree in only two years and pay only $10,000.00 for it. I become a highly sought-after job candidate. I double my income year after year. I buy a condo at age 25 with zero financial help from my parents. I write and publish a book that ends up getting over 100 reviews on Amazon. I create a YouTube channel that eventually amasses over a million lifetime views. I start a company and make enough money to hire two employees in the first year of business.

Change How You Tell Your Story

Once you change your current frame of reference, the second step is to change how you tell your story. My friend, Lily, who currently works in accounting, is in the middle of transitioning her career into filmmaking. She is working full time at a large accounting corporation where she feels boxed in by all the corporate rules. After work and on the weekends, she spends time writing a movie script. Lily told me about how she's scared that this movie will be a total flop, and that she's spending all her time and money on this but it'll lead to nothing. She's scared that if she pursues film, then ten years from now, she's going to be in a worse financial place than she is now, and she'll never be able to retire in her 60s.

Can you imagine what kind of energy Lily will give off when she's talking to investors, producers, actors, musicians, makeup artists, etc. about the vision she has for the film she wants to create? No one is going to believe in her vision enough to want to collaborate with her to make this a success. If she doesn't believe in her own vision, no one else will.

The future is unwritten. Anyone who claims to read your future is lying to you. Anyone who says that based on their experience, you will fail, is trying to play their hand at being God. You write your own future. Is there such a thing as predetermined destiny? I believe we have already decided many aspects of our life blueprint before even being born, but we still have a lot of leeway through free will. We have the agency to make decisions that alter the course of our lives.

Since you write your own future, you can choose to talk about it differently. What if Lily said to herself:

"My name is Lily. I moved all the way from China to the United States by myself to build my own American dream and pursue my happiness. I currently work full time as an accountant (*fact*). While I'm building my dream, I'm committed to writing a script for my new movie on the evenings and weekends (*fact*). This has been my dream for several years (*fact*) and I am now in the right life stage to do this (*subjective*).

"Because of my background in accounting, I have a big leg up over other people who went straight into the creative field. In understanding the financials (*fact*), I can use that as a strength. When pitching to investors, I can make sure this film stays within budget (*fact*).

"I've been gathering inspiration by watching other movies and paying attention to the color grading and composition of the shots (*fact*). I took a bunch of screenshots and saved them on my phone so I can find the common patterns and figure out what my personal style is for the films I want to make (*fact*). Right now, I'm working with another writer and I'm learning a lot about how to work with other people who differ greatly from me (*fact*). This is going to be an awesome film, and everyone is going to love it so much (*subjective*). This film will really move people and they'll remember it forever (*subjective*)."

How do you think people would react to Lily if she spoke to herself in this manner instead?

Notice how nothing has changed about Lily's life right now. What changed was how she talked about her life. My suggested version is more empowering. It has a bunch of powerful facts about what she's doing right now, mixed in with some subjective conclusions. The subjective conclusions are such because you cannot force outcomes and reactions. Since we do not know the outcomes, we can either say they will be great or will be poor. Outcomes are not within your control. You cannot control how other people feel about something. The only thing within your control is your own action (thoughts). You can only put your best effort into something to increase the likelihood of getting the outcome you want to achieve.

It's okay to lie to yourself in this way. People lie to themselves all the time. Ever met someone you thought was so incredibly amazing and beautiful, yet no matter how much you tried to convince them of that, they still had low self-esteem and believed they were a total loser? How could that person lie to himself? Everybody lies to themselves. They either keep telling themselves lies until it becomes true, or they keep hunting for all the evidence to prove that their lie is true. You can flip this psychological phenomenon into your favor by lying to yourself about how your future is going to be so amazing, and then one day it becomes true and it's no longer a lie.

Change Your Beliefs About Rejection

The third step to having confidence in your interview is to change your beliefs about rejection. You have to believe that if you don't get the job, that's the best outcome because that means you have a second chance at getting another opportunity that is a better fit for you.

Rejection isn't personal. I used to take rejection personally, as if there must be something wrong with me. "What is wrong with me?" When you ask yourself that kind of question, what do you expect your brain to answer? Your brain isn't going to answer, "There is nothing wrong with you." Your brain is a computer.

Your brain is going to list off all the things that might be wrong with you! Don't fall into that trap.

If you can talk to yourself in a way that says, "Rejection? Bring it on," you'll be much more confident in your interview.

I once saw a "help wanted" sign for a Deli Slicer position on the entrance door of CTown Supermarkets. I had been slicing deli meats and cheeses at another grocery store a few blocks away for six months. The guy asked me, "How much experience do you have?"

I told him, "Six months."

"You don't have enough experience to cut deli. You need at least one year of full-time experience to cut deli well."

Right... because operating a deli slicing machine is an extremely difficult skill to learn. You need to have done it for 2,080 hours to be good at it. Some people are so dense, they can't spot a good hire even if it was standing right there in their face. A week after he rejected me, a hardware store offered me a full-time bookkeeping job with zero relevant experience. That was the job that enabled me to finally move out of my parents' house at age 20.

When I first moved to Boston in 2018, I applied for a customer service job at ezCater. I did research on the company and really believed I would land an offer. I read an interview by the Founder/CEO. She wrote she liked to hire an eclectic sort of person who came from other industries and did different things because they bring a fresh perspective to the company. I thought, *I'm definitely different... I am an author and graduated college in only two years... I have the ability to create different solutions to existing problems. Plus, it's customer service and I've had a lot of training in communication skills.* I was really enthusiastic in my phone interview. There was no way I wouldn't be able to get this job.

I got rejected the next day. I asked the ezCater recruiter why. She said, "Based on how you spoke on the phone, you don't have what it takes to answer phones. Your phone communication skills are terrible." She was saying this to me, after I had worked at Domino's Pizza answering phones all day for a year and a half.

Annie Margarita Yang can't answer phones? She had poor judgment.

After my rejection from ezCater, I landed a job in real estate accounting where my talents were very much appreciated, and people loved my work so much that they fought to keep me. I was working in the real estate industry, which gave me the opportunity to attend lots of presentations given by mortgage lenders and learn about different first-time homebuyer programs I could qualify for.

If I had received the job offer from ezCater, I would have been part of their April 2020 layoff, where they cut over 400 of their 900 employees. I had been planning and saving for the down payment to buy a house for two years. If I had been part of a layoff like that, it would have affected my ability to get a mortgage because lenders want to see two years of continuous employment. I bought my condo in August 2020 when the interest rate was only 2.875%. My new monthly mortgage payment ended up being less than my rent. We will probably never see mortgage interest rates that low ever again. Everything worked out perfectly. The opportunity and timing were divine. I couldn't have predicted it would happen to me.

If you get rejected, it's really a blessing. You weren't meant to work there. There is a better path for you elsewhere. You just need to keep going. View that rejection as your practice interview to prepare you for the job you were really meant to land. When you're able to internalize this mindset, you'll be more at ease during your interview.

Show the Real You

Finally, be truthful about who you are in your interview. Don't pretend to be someone else and don't lie. Don't give answers you think the interviewer wants to hear. Be direct and honest about who you are. I meet so many people who think they have to put on a mask at work about who they are. When you hide behind a mask, you've erected a barrier that prevents you from connecting with others.

Nobody is perfect. To make mistakes is to be human. Interviewers don't expect job candidates to be perfect. That's imposing a double standard since they cannot meet that perfect standard themselves. What interviewers really want to know is what is your best and what is your worst? Have you done anything to work on those weaknesses?

Technically, you can land a job offer by being fake in your interview. People do it all the time and they get jobs. After they start the job, they can continue putting up this front, but the real person will always reveal itself, whether it's through offhand comments or mildly stressful situations that catch them off guard. When people discover the real you, they will resent you because they bought into your false advertising. You won't feel happy about your job once you realize you don't fit in. You should just be yourself in the interview (while still putting your best foot forward), and if they perceive the real you as being the right fit in the interview, chances are you'll also be the right fit at the company.

The Art of Following Up

Having navigated through the job seeking process, conducting yourself authentically in interviews, and dealing with rejections positively, it's crucial not to forget the final step: following up. The art of following up on job interviews can leave a lasting positive impression and potentially turn the tide in your favor. To help you get it right, I've developed a job interview follow-up email template that you can download at annieyangfinancial.com/post-interview-email. It's more than a mere courtesy; it's a proactive step to show your continued interest in the role and to stay on the recruiter's radar. Consider it a game-changer for your job search, offering a structured and professional way to emphasize your commitment and enthusiasm for the opportunity.

Chapter 48

Evaluating Job Offers Beyond
the Salary

Should you accept the job offer?

Don't be so quick to jump and say yes simply because the new job will pay more than your current job. I used to accept every opportunity. After getting burned a few times, I learned not every opportunity is worth my time. I always advocate for financial independence, and to get there, you have to make more money. However, financial independence also requires long-term thinking. I highly encourage you to think about and reflect on the following factors so that you can play your cards right:

Future Boss

How well did you click with your future boss in the interview? Your relationship with your boss determines your career within the company. Your boss will advocate for you, introduce you to the right people, and assign new opportunities and projects. You don't have to click with all your coworkers, but you definitely have to click with your boss.

Salary

Think long term about your career. Getting offered the high end of your pay range can feel great for now, but you've been capped. In order to get paid more in the future, the next step in your career would need to be getting promoted to a better title with more responsibilities. Would this kind of job be a good stepping stone for that promotion 2-3 years from now?

If you receive an offer from a company, and based on the budget, they really can't offer you more money, it's possible that the job has a lot of opportunities for your future growth, even though it doesn't pay as well as you'd like. You can request a better title while you do the same job duties. You can always learn the additional skills necessary for the better job title while working on the job. This move won't benefit you now as much as it will benefit you 2-3 years from now when you're looking for a new job.

Non-Compete Agreements

Non-compete agreements aren't necessarily a deal breaker. Check the law for your state regarding non-compete agreements to see whether they are enforceable. With non-compete agreements, you may not work for the competition at least one year after you resign from this job. Or, you can't work for the competition in a similar capacity, but if you were doing a completely different job for the competition, it would be okay. Or they could limit it to only competition within a certain geographic radius from the office.

I've been asked to sign a non-compete agreement with a 25-mile radius. I showed the company that 25 miles in all directions meant I couldn't work in Massachusetts! New Hampshire was only 20 miles away, for Christ's sake! I negotiated it down to 5 miles.

Someone else told me she accepted a job offer at a company and checked all the documents they asked her to sign before giving her notice of resignation. After signing the job offer, they asked her to sign a non-compete agreement. It was a very underhanded move. Based on what happened to her, I recommend you proactively ask the company if you're required to sign a non-compete agreement before signing the job offer and giving your two-week notice.

Happiness

The most important question is whether you'll be happy working there. High salary cannot make up for unhappiness. You can work a high salary job temporarily, but happiness does not stem from money. You can end up hating your job in six months. This is not sustainable. The stress from working a job you hate can create physical health problems that are challenging.

This wisdom comes from personal experience. I was so excited by the salary, I accepted the job and forgot to ask myself whether I'd be happy working alongside my new coworkers. My new coworkers turned out to be jealous and passive aggressive, undermining me at every step of the way when I tried to make improvements at doing my job. They liked everything the way it was before I started working there. Since I was so good at what I did, I highlighted their incompetence simply by being me.

It got to the point where they wouldn't even acknowledge my presence when I walked into the room. When I said, "good morning," they would roll their eyes. I tried so hard to be nice and professional and to make them like me, but I realized I would never fit in no matter how much I tried. Working there caused me to develop chronic acid reflux. It took me one year to get back to perfect health and I'm young. If I were older, I think it would have taken me even longer to recover.

Despite trying to avoid ending up in a job you hate, it's true that you can't completely avoid it. You can do all the research and due diligence, but you don't really know what the job and your coworkers will be like until after you work there. Just know that you're not stuck there. You don't have to stay if it ends up not being right for you. You can create and execute a plan to get a new and better job.

Also, if you end up in that situation, hindsight is 20/20. Instead of resisting it, I convince myself that my life was always meant to happen that way. I was meant to accept the job with the jealous and passive aggressive coworkers. Had I known beforehand, I wouldn't have accepted the job offer, and I wouldn't have developed all my amazing skills. It was the opportunity I needed. But I didn't need to stay, so I created my plans to leave after getting as much as I could out of the situation.

As you ponder all these factors, a great way to compare the pros and cons of each offer is to have them side by side. To aid in this, you can download the Job Offer Comparison Chart at an-nieyangfinancial.com/compare-offers.

Once you've made your decision and it's time to accept your job offer, you might find yourself unsure of how to best communicate your acceptance. To guide you through this process, you can download the Job Offer Acceptance Email Template at an-nieyangfinancial.com/accept-email.

Should You Hold Out for More Offers?

It depends on where you are in your career right now. I attended a Zoom Meetup for a local Financial Independence group. In the meetup, someone had just graduated college and asked for advice on how to approach his job search. He asked if he should only apply to jobs he thought were worthy of his time. He also asked if he should take the first job offer even if the pay was low, or should he hold out for something slightly higher paying?

Everyone in the group was much older (at least in their 30s) and told him to hold out for something slightly higher paying.

I don't think anyone in that group understood. I think they gave him poor advice. This young man has zero skills and experience in the work world. He doesn't have much power or leverage in negotiation. He can use the negotiation strategies, but he hasn't developed a proven track record of excellent performance.

It's much better to take the job you're offered, even if it's not great, and work your way up. You can even choose to take the job in order to pay your bills and continue applying for more jobs over the next few months until you land something better. You're working an entry-level job. No one is expecting you to stay for long anyway.

Everyone starts out at entry level. It might not seem like it, but it's a pretty even playing field in the beginning. The real difference starts to show in five years. If you play your cards right over the course of five years, you'll end up in a better place than most other people who graduated at the same time.

If you follow the advice from that FI group, you don't know how long you'll have to wait until you're finally offered something better. It could be a few months. In those few months, how will you pay your bills? Are your parents funding you? But if you don't have parents to support you financially to hold out for something much better, what are you going to do? Are you going to dig yourself into debt? You'll need to pay all the debt back after you finally get that better-paying job. Financially, you'd be worse off even though the income is slightly higher. A slightly higher income doesn't offset the difficulty of paying off all the debt, especially if you owe student loans.

Chapter 49

Designing and Creating Your Dream Life

"There are many flowers in my father's garden, and many gardens in my father's house."

—*Robert Guddahl*

The only thing stopping you from having everything you want in life is your belief that you can't do it, and that you can't have it. It doesn't matter where you start. It doesn't matter what kind of family you were born into, which schools you attended, what your childhood was like, or what happened in your past. The only thing that matters is where you're going, and what you believe your future will be like.

There are tons of stories of real-life people who were born into poverty and accomplished great things in life. Those people weren't special. They were normal people, just like you and me. The difference is in how they reacted to their circumstances. This is why two children with the same parents can have completely different life trajectories despite having the same upbringing. The children each reacted differently. It's the reason poor children can become rich adults and why rich children can lose it all in adulthood. It is your attitude and your personal philosophy that sets the sail toward the future you create.

Everything you see today was first created in someone's mind. The circumstance was the soil, the thought was the seed, and the emotion was the water. Given enough time, you end up with a tree. Look around you. All the furniture in your house was designed in someone's mind first before getting manufactured. An architect designed the house after a real estate developer had the thought of building a new house and followed through on making it a reality. Every little thing you see around you, from the traffic lights to the roads, and the cars, was conceived in the mind before being created into something tangible.

You can apply the same system to create a life where you can land a job offer in five days. It all begins with your belief that it is possible. For many years, I had to work on the mindset as the foundation before anything tangible came into existence. It was frustrating because the environment and the surrounding circumstances did not match the results I wanted and the vision I had in my head. I kept planting tons of seeds and watering all of them until one day some of them grew into seedlings. Then, some of those seedlings became full trees that bore fruit. It required a lot of patience.

The Heart's Desire List

The daily exercise I did for two years was called the Heart's Desire List. Missouri State Senator Brian Nieves introduced it to me at a workshop when I was 20 years old. It was the first time I was in the presence of someone so successful (he's successful enough to have a Wikipedia page...) so I genuinely valued what he had to teach.

The Heart's Desire List exercise is simple. You make a list of your affirmations and every single day, on a fresh sheet of paper, keep writing the same affirmations. To hold myself accountable, I would write the day # at the top right corner of the paper and keep it until the next day. The next day, I would write the new day # and throw out yesterday's paper. I did this to make sure I never skipped a day by accident. After a few months of doing this, the affirmations became automatic and ingrained in my mind. At first, the thoughts felt unnatural and forced. But later, those thoughts would naturally come into my mind throughout the day while I was running errands. When that happens, you know you've successfully planted the new thoughts.

Here are the same affirmations I used all those years ago. You should create your own. I created these from scratch based on the personal struggles I had. You'll see that my list was really long. I started with only five affirmations, but as I realized I had so many personal challenges to overcome, I kept adding more to my list. This exercise took me around 20 minutes a day to complete every morning before breakfast.

1. I am confident, charismatic, and influential around everyone I meet.
2. I am a social butterfly who constantly listens to and validates others.
3. I am surrounded by a loving community.
4. I am only three degrees of separation away from everyone in the world.
5. I am always lucky, meeting the right people, at the right place, at the right time.
6. I have a bubble around me that blocks out naysayers, and all their reasonableness gets reflected back at them 10x more.
7. I know how to say "no" to people.
8. I negotiate win-win situations all the time with ease.
9. I am a natural giver and receiver.
10. I enjoy eating only healthy foods that are energetically in tune with me and nourish my body and voice.
11. I avoid sugar, corn, gluten, chocolate, beef, and dairy every day. (I'm allergic to these foods. I had to teach myself to enjoy life without these foods in my diet forever.)
12. I drink 8 cups of water every day.

13. My skin is clear, young, beautiful, healthy, flawless, regenerative, and even toned.

14. I sleep every day before midnight and wake up 7-8 hours later refreshed and ready to take on the world.

15. I enjoy exercising my body and voice so that it is healthy and strong.

16. I breathe and relax deeply and I let go of small issues and unneeded stress.

17. I respect myself, my body, and my time.

18. I trust my intuition, which always leads me down the higher path.

19. I acknowledge my skills and talents and am proud of all my accomplishments, achievements, and hard work.

20. I use my time productively, wisely, and efficiently, and only do activities beneficial for my career, health and wellbeing, and friends and family.

21. I am Annie Yang and I am the best fucking speaker of all time.

22. I write every day and my writing is clear, concise, excellent, and transforms lives.

23. I make money providing tremendous value to people and adding to their lives.

24. I am prosperous, abundant, and manifest every positive dream and goal instantly.

25. I remove all resistances to making money so that money flows to me freely from all sources.

26. I am a moneymaking and idea machine.

27. My happiness is not grounded upon and dependent on someone else's behavior.

28. I have a romantic, interdependent relationship with Handrio and continue to be happy no matter what he does.

29. I intuitively know how to proceed in my relationship with Handrio.

30. I have a healthy relationship toward sex and enjoy and feel comfortable with physical intimacy. (It took me three years to fully overcome the foot fetish trauma.)

Ladder Thoughts

Lately, I've been examining the limiting beliefs I have surrounding learning piano as an adult.

One of the limiting beliefs I had was "I can't sing." Seven years ago, I moved in with my husband. I did vocal exercises when I was home alone one day. I thought I had some time before my husband came back home from school, but he came home early from the 2nd entrance he never used. He listened to me sing through the door and then opened the door and burst out laughing. I was so embarrassed that I never sang again for seven years. Prior to moving in with him, I really enjoyed singing but after that day, I believed "I can't sing."

Because of a hand injury, I couldn't play piano at my piano lessons, so my teacher made me sing instead. I felt extremely uncomfortable. She said I could sing, so why was I so afraid? I repressed the memory of my husband laughing at me and suddenly that day, I remembered the source of my limiting belief.

I let this one limiting belief dictate my life for the last seven years. I needed to work on this belief because the only way I could get better at piano is by singing. I need to feel the music in my body, and sing the music, before I can play the music on the piano.

But how can I go from "I can't sing" to "I can sing"? It's too much of a jump and no matter how much I repeat to myself that "I can sing," I won't believe it because it doesn't have an ounce of truth in it.

The solution is to use an in-between thought.

"I am choosing to believe I can sing," is a true statement.

I am repeating, "I am choosing to believe I can sing" until it feels comfortable and true before I move onto saying, "I can sing."

With the thought, "I am choosing to believe I can sing," I've had a much easier time practicing singing every day and I am making progress in my sight-singing skills.

You can create ladder thoughts using these templates:

- I am learning to...
- Even though.... It's possible I can....
- I'm open to...
- I'm looking forward to...
- It's possible that...
- I'm willing to consider...
- I'm on my way to...
- I'm choosing to believe...
- I'm in the process of...

For example, in my case, my ladder thoughts for learning piano would be:

- I am learning to sight sing.
- Even though music theory is difficult, it's possible I am capable of learning it.
- I'm open to playing the piano in public with confidence.
- I'm looking forward to playing the piano at an advanced level.
- It's possible that I can become a professional pianist starting as an adult.
- I'm willing to consider the possibility that I can make this dream come true.
- I'm on my way to becoming a professional musician.
- I'm choosing to believe I can sing.
- I'm in the process of doing everything a professional musician had to do to get to where they are.

100 Reasons Why You Can

I discovered a new exercise that I am trying out to remove my limiting beliefs. I cannot guarantee that it works because I haven't seen the results for myself yet, but a successful person said that it worked for him. I only take advice from successful people already doing what I want to accomplish, so if it worked for him, there's a high chance it would work for me and you as well.

You fill in the blank every single day with a new reason for why you can achieve something. Our minds can easily come up with reasons why you can't do something on autopilot. You need to teach your mind to do the opposite by training your mind to come up with reasons why you can. It will disrupt the autopilot that your mind runs on.

Using my piano example, "I can learn piano as an adult because... ___"

- Day 1: I can learn piano as an adult because I have a lot of discipline.
- Day 2: I can learn piano as an adult because I never miss a single piano lesson.
- Day 3: I can learn piano as an adult because I practice for two hours a day.
- Day 4: I can learn piano as an adult because I've always accomplished what I set my mind to doing, and this is no different.
- Day 5: I can learn piano as an adult because I have an amazing teacher.
- Day 6: I can learn piano as an adult because I have access to a variety of resources.
- Day 7: I can learn piano as an adult because I am a quick learner in everything I wanted to learn.
- Day 8: I can learn piano as an adult because I have a growth mindset.
- Day 9: I can learn piano as an adult because I am extremely committed.
- Day 10: I can learn piano as an adult because Albert Franz is an example of someone who did it already.
- Day 11: I can learn piano as an adult because I have made a lot of progress already so there is my proof.
- Day 12: I can learn piano as an adult because I will never give up.

You can apply the same exercise using the statement, "I can land a job offer in five days because... _____" After one year, you'll have 365 reasons why you can accomplish this.

I would like to close with the Gateway Affirmation.

I am more than my physical body, because I am more than physical matter.

Always remember, you are eternal.

God created you in his image.

You are a creator.

What will you create with your life?

Share Your Thoughts:
Leave a Review

Your Opinion Matters! I would truly appreciate hearing your thoughts about my book. In the world of book publishing, honest reviews from diverse readers hold immense value. By sharing your review, you'll help prospective readers determine if this book is right for them. Additionally, your valuable feedback will boost the visibility of my book and enable me to reach a broader audience.

Please go to annieyangfinancial.com/job-review to share your review, and thank you for your support!

About The Author

Annie Margarita Yang is the go-to finance guru for Millennials refusing to lose in a system stacked against them. A candid, no-fluff YouTube personality and best selling author of 1,001 Ways to Save Money and The 5-Day Job Search, Annie is a part of the group she educates—the demographic most misunderstood because they must overcome finance challenges previous generations didn't.

She is skilled at creating easy-to-follow money saving systems, intentional in addressing the unique concerns of Millennials, and relentless about creating financial independence.

With more than 1 million views on YouTube, her witty approach to tough talk sets her apart from others.

An accountant by trade but most passionate about personal finance, Annie dodged student loan debt by leaping into the world of minimum wage jobs after high school. She grew a love for frugal living, self-education, and planning for the future during those years. Annie understood that while it wasn't easy to avoid debt, it was possible. She later earned her B.A. in Communications from Thomas Edison State University.

By day, Annie works as an accounting manager and business operations leader in the real estate industry. By night, she gives her all to help others overcome the biggest obstacle of their lives. She specializes in saving money and helping people free up funds in their budgets for the things that truly matter in life.

Annie lives with her husband in Boston, where she is fully committed to learning the piano!

Also By The Author

Discover more valuable insights and practical advice from the author in her other book:

1001 Ways to Save Money: Quit Flushing Your Hard-Earned Money Down the Toilet

Tired of watching your hard-earned money go down the drain? This comprehensive guide offers you 1001 practical tips and tricks to save money in every aspect of your life. From everyday expenses to long-term financial goals, this book will help you keep more of your money where it belongs—in your wallet.

Don't miss out on this opportunity to transform your financial future. Get your copy of 1001 Ways to Save Money today!

Available now on Amazon.

annieyangfinancial.com/save-money